PR.

SOU

"Reading Frank's teachings is like sitting at the feet of a master. *Soul Food* provides a fantastic opportunity to learn from someone who knows the way — and is generous enough to share it with us."

— BOB BURG
Coauthor of *The Go-Giver* and *The Go-Giver Influencer*

"*Soul Food* will help you excel as an extraordinary individual and ethical leader. I wish I had this book long ago. I strongly recommend reading it!"

— PROFESSOR M.S. RAO, PhD
Father of "Soft Leadership" and author of over 40 leadership books

"*Soul Food* provides the recipe for a happier, more meaningful life, with better relationships and greater success. These nuggets of relatable, easy-to-digest wisdom will inspire the best in you."

— MELANIE GREENBERG, PhD
Clinical psychologist, coach, and author of *The Stress-Proof Brain*

"Frank Sonnenberg serves the world, leading us to perform our best in life and work. *Soul Food* is an outstanding compendium of actionable inspiration that will add value in any setting."

— JAMES STROCK
Author of *Serve to Lead*

"If you only have time to read one book this decade, make it *Soul Food*. It is not a book to be read. It is a recipe to be lived."

— AUGUST TURAK
Templeton Prize-winning author of *Brother John: A Monk, a Pilgrim and the Purpose of Life*

PRAISE FOR
SOUL FOOD

"*Soul Food* is truly a life-changing book. It's filled with incredible wisdom and practical advice that will help you achieve a new level of success and happiness."

— JOHN SPENCE
Named "Among Top 500 Leadership Development Experts in the World" by HR.com

"*Soul Food* promotes nurturing from the inside out. Frank Sonnenberg offers concise and actionable tips to help you think about the most important things in life."

— LARAE QUY
Former counterintelligence FBI agent, author of *Mental Toughness for Women Leaders* and *Secrets of a Strong Mind*

"Frank Sonnenberg has a way of communicating powerful ideas in gentle ways. *Soul Food* provides inspirational lessons that will help you live the life of your dreams. It's a must-read."

— SARAH HINER
President and CEO, Bottom Line Inc. (Publisher of *Bottom Line Personal*)

"When Frank says, 'for what it's worth,' it's your clue to listen up! There's a gem of wisdom that follows this humble phrase. *Soul Food* — Read it. Be inspired. For what it's worth…"

— SHARON TELESCA FEURER
Luxury hospitality consultant and business strategist

"Frank Sonnenberg offers the greatest wisdom and penetrating insights of any author I have ever read. *Soul Food* is his best."

— BOB VANOUREK
Award-winning leadership author and the former CEO of five companies

SOUL FOOD

Change Your Thinking, Change Your Life

FRANK SONNENBERG

Printed in the United States of America.

ISBN-13: 978-1726290500
ISBN-10: 1726290506

CreateSpace, North Charleston, SC

Cover and interior design by Carrie Ralston, Simple Girl Design LLC.

To my wife, and best friend, Caron
— Love doesn't have an expiration date.

and

To Catherine, Eric, Kristine, and John
— Be a good person.
Everything else is secondary.

CONTENTS

ACKNOWLEDGMENTS

The goal of this book is to share valuable lessons to boost your happiness and success. Two quotes contained within these pages capture the essence of this book quite well:

"It's not what you *have*, but who you *are* that counts."

"Ability determines if you *can*; attitude determines if you *will*."

I'd like to recognize several people who were instrumental in creating this book. Words cannot express my gratitude for their support. They are incredibly talented, have an amazing work ethic, and are a pleasure to work with. Most importantly, they embody the values that are depicted in this book. That is very important to me.

Caron Sonnenberg is my best friend and the love of my life. Caron is the first person to review each essay, and she makes editorial comments and suggestions to enhance each one. She also recommends new topics to consider and offers her perceptive viewpoint. Caron's ideas and comments are always insightful and very much appreciated. Thank you, Caron, for your tremendous support and encouragement in creating this book.

Carrie Ralston, Simple Girl Design, is incredibly gifted. I've worked with many art directors over the years. Carrie is clearly among the best. She's talented, takes great pride in her work, and has an attitude that's second to none. Thank you, Carrie.

Kathy Dix is the consummate professional. Even though I've worked with Kathy for years, I continue to be in awe of her expertise. Kathy is a knowledgeable, insightful, and meticulous proofreader. I've come to rely heavily on her sage advice. This book would not have been possible without her. Thank you, Kathy.

Eric Wagner, Fifth Cup LLC, is knowledgeable, experienced, and responsive. He works his technology magic so that our blog always runs smoothly. I can always get a good night's sleep knowing that Eric is at the helm. His passion, work ethic, and responsiveness are in a class of their own. Thank you, Eric.

. . .

I feel like I'm the luckiest guy in the world. I have a wonderful family, fantastic friends, a fairytale marriage, and an awesome career. What more can a guy want? I owe much of my success and happiness to those wonderful people in my life. For that I am forever grateful.

I am a student of life. As I say, "Life is a classroom." I've always searched for better ways to do things and sought feedback on how to become a better person. There have been many folks, too many to mention here, who have been kind enough to take me under their wing, mentor me, offer constructive feedback, and show me the ropes. The lessons they taught me have been priceless.

There are a few special people I'd like to recognize who have been extremely instrumental in shaping my character and in making my life rewarding and meaningful. My friends Dr. Mark Sandberg, David Tierno, Larry Frankel, Denis Salamone, and Ed Berryman all have something in common: They have strong moral character, they've enjoyed outstanding careers, and they are exceptional role models.

These folks clearly raise the bar for others to follow. They are incredibly accomplished and yet they're humble, have demanding schedules and yet they maintain balance. Although they're always on the run, they find time to make a difference. They're genuinely good people, admired and respected by many, and are living proof that good people do finish first. The world is a better place because of them — my world certainly is.

My mother and father were wonderful role models who instilled the strong values in me that are so much a part of this book. My brothers and I grew up in a household where honesty and integrity presided over all else, where people's wealth was measured by their character rather than their material possessions, and where people got more joy from giving than from asking for more. My parents fled Germany during the Hitler regime. They didn't complain about what life dealt them because they knew they were lucky to make it safely to America. Like many others, they had hopes of building a life for their family and living the American Dream. They instilled in us the confidence that we could be anyone or do anything as long as we had the courage and the will to achieve our dreams.

Caron and I raised our girls, Catherine and Kristine, to be kind and generous, to find their purpose in life, and to take great pleasure in life's journey. We're so proud of them. There's nothing more gratifying than watching your kids grow up to become thoughtful and productive members of society. One of the best indicators of their value system is the men they chose to marry. Caron and I can't say enough good things about Eric and John. They're ambitious, principled, and kind. Most of all, they know what matters and have a wonderful perspective about life. Girls…You did good. :)

Caron and I had our first date June 19, 1978. Two years later we got married. It's amazing how much impact one person can have on my life. We raised a family, built a business together, and have literally (and I mean, literally) spent every waking hour together. And yet, I still don't get tired of being in her company. I thought of Caron when I wrote the quote, "Love has no expiration date." The fact is, my life wouldn't be complete without her. Our wedding dance was "I love you just the way you are." That was true then, and it's still true today.

I'd like to give a quick shout-out to all the folks who read, comment, and share my blog posts each day. At the time of publishing, *FrankSonnenbergOnline* has an audience of over two million people. It's not a business; it's my passion. Thank YOU for helping me make a difference by spreading the word that moral character matters.

Thank you all! :)

ABILITY
DETERMINES
IF YOU CAN;
ATTITUDE
DETERMINES
IF YOU WILL.

— FRANK SONNENBERG

THERE'S ONLY ONE
INVESTMENT
THAT WILL NEVER
GO DOWN —
AN INVESTMENT
IN YOURSELF.

INTRODUCTION: WHAT'S THE BEST INVESTMENT THAT YOU CAN MAKE?

What's the best investment you can make? Some people invest in hard assets such as stocks, bonds, and real estate; others invest in collectibles. But there's a better alternative. Let me give you a hint: It can't be taxed; it can't be reduced by inflation; and it won't wear out or depreciate, like driving a new car out of the showroom. Furthermore, it'll enrich your life and make it more rewarding in untold ways. The fact is, there's only one investment that will never go down — an investment in yourself.

Some people intuitively know that personal development is critical, but they either feel they've spent lots of years in school, think they can't find the time, or think they already know everything there is to know about everything. So personal development is relegated to the backburner.

Those who think that learning is over upon graduation are sadly mistaken. As Albert Einstein said, "Wisdom is not a product of schooling but of the lifelong attempt to acquire it." There are five critical areas that you should address. They are:

building a reservoir of *knowledge*,
mastering critical *skills*,
gaining valuable *experience*,
forming a beneficial *mindset*,
and developing a strong *moral character*.

NEVER BE TOO BUSY TO LEARN

Build a reservoir of knowledge. Just because you have unlimited access to information these days doesn't guarantee you're benefitting from it. It's important to be curious, discerning, open-minded, and careful that the information you receive is of high quality — credible, accurate, objective, comprehensive, and of course, relevant in some way. Everything you learn is like money in the bank.

Master critical skills. Skills are tools that you use to apply your knowledge. Examples include critical thinking, problem solving, interpersonal communication, stress reduction, and time management. It's important to refine your skills by always remembering that practice makes perfect. Conversely, practice doesn't make perfect if you're doing it wrong.

Gain valuable life experience. Professional development shouldn't be limited to formal work experience; you can learn as much from playing a sport or learning to play a musical instrument. The truth is, performing the activity isn't what counts; it's the know-how gained from the encounter. You'll learn valuable lessons every time you leave your comfort zone, set stretch goals, accept feedback, reflect on your experience, and learn from mistakes and failures.

Form a beneficial mindset. Every experience that you have will shape your mindset and your view of the world. You'll learn such things as the power of positive thinking, how to face adversity, the importance of determination, how to confront your weaknesses, and how to rebound from disappointment.

Develop a strong moral character. Senator Alan Simpson said it well, "If you have integrity, nothing else matters. If you don't have integrity, nothing else matters."

Personal development is a building process in which all the aha moments that you have are cumulative — and are added to your toolkit.

MAKE THE INVESTMENT — STRIVE TO BECOME A BETTER YOU

Some folks don't make the effort to better themselves. They wake up disillusioned after years of inattention and neglect and realize the world has passed them by. This often leads to frustration, resentment, and even anger. The fact is, you can't treat personal development like going on a crash diet for being out of shape. Personal development is a continuous building process that requires time, effort, and personal commitment. If you think the world is going to stand still because you're not interested or motivated to make an investment in yourself, you're sadly mistaken; unless you learn something new every day, you're becoming obsolete. Learning is as much an attitude as it is an activity. If you don't make the commitment, don't complain about the outcome. Take a few moments each week to invest in yourself. You'll be glad you did. It's the best investment you can make.

You've taken the first step in investing in yourself by buying this book. It's not necessarily designed to read in order, but you can do so if you'd like. Determine how each lesson applies to you. Identify ideas that you'd like to implement. And, most importantly, act on them. Enjoy! :)

"

YOUR MINDSET MATTERS MORE THAN YOU THINK.

— FRANK SONNENBERG

ONE OF THE BEST
WAYS TO FIND
SATISFACTION
IS TO
GIVE IT AWAY.

DO YOU HAVE A HEALTHY MINDSET?

Think about all the time that you spend taking care of your body: the organic food, the vitamin supplements, and, who can forget — the exercise. Do you focus the same amount of attention on your attitude, outlook, and self-confidence? The fact is, your mindset and view of the world can have a significant impact on your health and relationships, as well as on your success and happiness. It's time to nurture your frame of mind, too.

You are limited by your thoughts. While some of your thinking is constructive, other times it's detrimental, actively working against you. There are specific things you can do to make your mindset work for you rather than against you.

GET IN THE RIGHT FRAME OF MIND

Give your mindset a workout. Take a moment each day to ensure that your mindset is actively serving your best interests. Here are 13 factors to serve as guideposts.

Identify things to be thankful for. Are you grateful for what you have or do you take things for granted? Take a moment to appreciate the wonderful things in your life.

Dance through life. Do you put the best face on things or complain all the time? Happiness is contagious…pass it on. As Dale Carnegie said, "Act enthusiastic, and you will be enthusiastic."

See the bright side. Do you see the glass as half-full or half-empty? Choose to see the positive side, today.

Challenge yourself. Do you embrace new opportunities or let your fears stop you from reaching your true potential? Step out of your comfort zone and go for it.

Do yourself proud. Do you do your best or settle for mediocrity? Excellence is not a destination, but a way of life.

Make the first move. Do you give freely or wait for others to go first? Give of yourself without expecting something in return. One of the best ways to find satisfaction is to give it away.

Show your gratitude. Do you show your appreciation or ignore other people's kindness and support? Take a moment to show how much you care.

Learn something new. Do you learn something new every day or hang onto old ways? Everyone likes routines; learn by breaking some of yours.

Take a five-minute vacation. Do you add to your busy schedule or find ways to eliminate unnecessary tasks? Use your extra time to practice mindfulness, meditation, or yoga.

Purge bad thoughts and emotions. Do uplifting or negative thoughts fill your head each day? Every time you feel anger, jealousy, or hate coming on, tell yourself, "Not today."

See the good in people. Do you focus on people's strengths or obsess over their weaknesses? Compliment someone. It'll make them feel good. And it'll make you feel good, too.

Reflect back on your day. Do you learn your lessons through experience or repeat your mistakes? Take a moment to reflect on your actions. Pause… and learn, before marching on.

Give yourself a pat on the back. Do you celebrate your wins or belittle yourself? Identify a couple of wins each day and give yourself an attaboy. You deserve it.

CHANGING YOUR MINDSET
IS A GAME CHANGER

We have a tendency to accentuate the negative rather than the positive. This is an evolutionary survival skill that we learned to help us avoid danger lurking around the bend. The problem is, if we permit negativity to overpower our thoughts — the power of suggestion will ultimately drag us down.

The best way to nurture your frame of mind is to turn the tables on negativity. Get into the habit of seeing the world through rose-colored glasses, of counting your blessings, and of being kind and generous to others. See the best, expect the best, and be the best. That's looking on the bright side. Are you up for the challenge? You have a healthy body… nurture a healthy mindset, too. :)

"

YOU GET WHAT
YOU EXPECT.

GREAT THINGS START WITH GREAT EXPECTATIONS

For years, athletes tried and failed to run a mile in less than four minutes. It was said that doing so would cause significant damage to a runner's health. However, on May 6, 1954, Roger Bannister set out to prove everyone wrong. To everyone's amazement, he broke the four-minute barrier, running the distance in 3:59.4 — breaking a record that had stood for nine years. Bannister taught us a valuable lesson. As part of his training, he set high expectations for himself and relentlessly visualized his success to create certainty in his mind.

It's interesting to note that as soon as Bannister proved a four-minute mile was feasible, it suddenly became possible for many others to achieve the same feat. In fact, even though "sub-four" continues to be a notable time for running the mile, top international runners routinely accomplish this achievement. The bottom line is that when you believe something's possible, it becomes possible.

This is true in all walks of life. For example, expectations are well recognized in medicine, where doctors have known the power of the placebo effect for a long time. The fact is, when people expect a particular outcome, they look for evidence to support their view. This can have a powerful effect on behavior and ultimately, on results.

HOW YOUR EXPECTATIONS BECOME
YOUR REALITY

People adjust their behavior based on the way they see the world. Here are 11 ways that expectations can affect your life every day:

If you believe **today's going to be awesome,** you're going to be happier and more productive than if you fear problems lurking around every corner.

If you believe **people are trustworthy,** you're going to manage relationships differently than if you think everyone's out to get you.

If you believe **you can overcome any challenge,** you're going to view obstacles differently than if you feel you're doomed from the start.

If you believe **you're going to be successful,** you're going to view your prospects differently than if you think, "People like me never stand a chance."

If you believe **relationships should be win-win,** you're going to build partnerships differently than if you think everyone's out to get the upper hand.

If you believe **good people finish first,** you're going to behave differently than if you think you have to be ruthless to win.

If you believe **feedback is critical to personal growth,** you're going to receive it differently than if you think feedback means you did something wrong.

If you believe **every successful person encounters failure**, you're going to view mistakes differently than if you think failing makes you a failure.

If you believe **hard work pays off**, you're going to view tough days differently than if you believe your company's trying to take advantage of you.

If you believe **people generally try their best**, you're going to manage people differently than if you think people are generally lazy.

If you believe **life has its ups and downs**, you're going to view bad days differently than if you think you're the only one with problems.

YOU GET WHAT YOU EXPECT

Expectations are everything! If you shoot for the moon, and fall a little short, you'll still end up among the stars. Conversely, some people set the bar so low you can trip over it. The fact is, "I can't" and "I won't" trigger the same results.

When you believe something's possible and you set your sights firmly on the prize, you've taken the first big step in making it a reality. When every part of you believes that the outcome will be positive, something magical happens. Great accomplishments begin with great expectations. You get what you expect. :)

'I CAN'T' AND
'I DON'T WANT TO'
TRIGGER THE
SAME RESULTS.

YOU CAN'T FORCE PEOPLE TO CARE

There's great truth in the saying, "You either have it or you don't." It's certainly true when it comes to the skills required to succeed. Some people choose to fail. (Yes, you read that right.)

Some folks *lack the skills* to get ahead, but others suffer from a *poor attitude*. Skills are *acquired*; attitude is a *choice*. The outcome, nevertheless, is still the same — failure. You can't force anyone to care. "I can't" and "I don't want to" trigger the same results.

ARE YOU HOLDING YOURSELF BACK?

Do you have the right attitude? Here are 15 phrases that expose people with a poor attitude.

"What's in it for me?" Are you selfless or do you focus primarily on *your* needs and wants? Greed can be the unwillingness to give *or* the willingness to take.

"You don't expect *me* to do that!" People will test you in small ways before trusting you with additional responsibility. Before you dine from a silver platter, you must first eat from a paper plate.

"They don't pay me enough to do this." Watch out. Excuses can be habit forming. Pull out the weeds or make peace with the dandelions.

"I don't feel like working today." Endurance is as much mental as it is physical. If you're not willing to make the commitment, don't complain about the outcome.

"Tuesday's going to be tough. I'm calling in sick." Some people will do anything to get out of work. Self-pity is like a disease — the condition worsens with neglect.

"I'm not checking my work. They'll catch mistakes during the review process." Make yourself proud. If it's worth your doing, give it all you're worth.

"I've always done it this way." Excuses proclaim an unwillingness to learn. Unless you learn something new every day, you're becoming obsolete.

"I hate doing that. Give it to someone else." No one likes to do menial work, but it comes with the territory. When you swallow your pride, don't choke on your ego.

"If I look busy, maybe I can get out of the work." Being busy doesn't mean that you're productive. Just because you're at work doesn't mean you're working.

"I'll do anything to get ahead." Character is the fingerprint of your soul. Everything has a price, but not everything should be for sale.

"Nobody's here, so we can goof off." If you're not responsible for your actions, who is? Listen to your conscience. That's why you have one.

"Nobody knows what they're doing around here." Those who love to find fault in others rarely find fault in themselves. People who can, do. People who can't, criticize.

"I hate it here." Be positive. If work isn't fun, you're not playing on the right team.

"I do what I have to — nothing more, nothing less." Be the best you can be — and then be a little better. Always give 110%. It's the extra 10% that everyone remembers.

"Three hours 'til I can go home." Watching the clock doesn't make time go faster. If you want to share in the rewards, share in the work.

A PERSON WITH NO COMMITMENT HAS NO PROMISE

There are two kinds of mistakes. First, despite our best efforts, we make a poor choice or misjudgment — nobody's perfect. For the most part, people are forgiving if you make an honest mistake or have a bad day on occasion. But when improper actions are *intentional*, trust will diminish and your reputation will suffer as a result. The same holds true for your attitude. It's one thing to lack the skills required to succeed, yet quite another to let a poor attitude cause your demise. The first type of mistake, a poor choice or misjudgment, is *unintentional*, while a poor attitude is a deliberate *choice*.

You can accomplish anything you set your mind to. Be positive. Reach for the stars and show that you care. Others can stop you for a moment. Only you can stop yourself for good. :)

IF YOU LOOK
FOR PROBLEMS
HARD ENOUGH,
YOU'RE BOUND
TO FIND ONE.

HOW DO YOU SEE THE WORLD AROUND YOU?

Do you view the glass as half-full or half-empty? I hope you said "neither" — it's never good to see the world through a single filter. Unfortunately, we often fall victim to "thinking traps" that influence our feelings and impact our behavior. It's not a matter of lacking intelligence, but rather of being blinded by a filter that distorts our thinking process. What you see depends on what you look for. For example, if you wake up thinking that today's going to be awesome, you'll likely be happier and more productive than if you fear that problems are lurking around every corner. If you look for problems hard enough, you're bound to find one.

The key is to know how you see the world and to manage it accordingly. Do these 20 behavioral filters sound familiar?

Mental filter. Some folks have blinders on. They view situations from one perspective — they're unable or unwilling to see other viewpoints.

Black or white. Some people focus on extremes and exclude everything in-between. They see everything as good or bad, right or wrong, all or nothing.

Overgeneralization. Some folks turn a *single* situation into a sweeping generalization. They assume that because "one teacher is lazy," the whole school is terrible.

Labeling. Some people label the whole group based on the behavior of a few members.

Jumping to conclusions. Some folks reach a conclusion without any evidence to support their claim.

Magnifying. Some people blow things out of proportion by magnifying the positive and minimizing the negative — or vice versa. This can be taken to extremes. "I made a mistake, so my life is over."

Half-truth. Some folks focus on half of the equation and ignore the other half. For example, they focus on the *discount* and lose sight of the *cost* of a purchase.

One way. Some people think it's their way or the highway. They expect others to conform to their way of thinking. Period.

Entitlement. Some folks believe rules that apply to others shouldn't apply to them.

Self-worth. Some people *overstate* the value of something simply because it's theirs. "My kid is a superstar. She should play the whole game."

Emotional reasoning. Some folks make their *feelings* their reality. "I'm afraid, so it must be dangerous."

Victimization. Some people feel helpless. They believe life isn't fair — the outcome is predetermined. "It doesn't pay to try."

Fortune telling. Some folks think they can predict the future; they use that view as the basis for their actions and decisions.

Mind reading. Some people believe they know what others are thinking — even if they don't have evidence.

Idealism. Some folks view the world through rose-colored glasses — the way it *should be* becomes their *reality*.

Conformity. Some people jump on the bandwagon; they accept the views of others with little or no thought.

Denial. Some folks feel so strongly about an issue that they wall themselves off from information that threatens their view.

Blame. Some people blame others for their misfortune. Conversely, others blame themselves for everything.

Self-doubt. Some folks turn a positive experience into a negative one. If they win an award, they're likely to say, "I didn't really deserve it. I probably won because…"

Righteous. Some people always have to be right.

Are any of these filters distorting your thinking process? When you see things through a rigid *filter*, it influences your mood, colors your decisions, and shades your outlook. In fact, it'll impact the way you view the world. The truth is, your perception becomes your reality. How do you see the world around you? :)

"

IF YOU BELIEVE
YOU CAN'T,
YOU WON'T.

DO YOU HAVE A VICTIM MENTALITY?

Even though some folks make their success look easy, it rarely is. The truth is, success in almost anything requires hard work, determination, and a positive mental attitude. But some people are their own worst enemy: they hurt themselves in ways they never imagined. The fact is, one of the biggest obstacles to success lies within each of us. Do you have a victim mentality?

Before you say "no," how often do you say, "Other people have it easier," "Why does this only happen to me?" or "I can't do anything right." Your outlook can work *for* you or *against* you…it's your choice.

SYMPTOMS OF A VICTIM MENTALITY

Negative habits produce negative results. Here are seven characteristics of a victim mentality:

Feeling powerless and helpless. Some people feel they don't have control over their situation. So they don't even try to affect the outcome.

Dwelling on negativity. Some folks complain about their tough life just to attract attention or to fill a void in conversation.

Generating self-abuse. Some people continually put themselves down.

Remaining stuck in the past. Some folks refuse to let go of disappointments.

Blaming the world. Some people blame scapegoats for their difficulties and setbacks.

Being consumed by problems. Some folks wear their problems as a badge of honor.

Feeling cheated. Some people are envious and resentful. They believe that "the world isn't fair."

11 WAYS TO ESCAPE A VICTIM MENTALITY

Playing the victim card is counterproductive. Here are 11 points to counteract that behavior:

Own your life. Accept responsibility for your past, present, and future. Don't outsource that responsibility to others.

Be positive. Focus on controlling your negative thinking. Mentally limit the times that you judge, complain, mistrust, or are jealous of others.

Believe in yourself. Do things that foster confidence and self-esteem. That includes recognizing your strengths and being kind to yourself.

Look in the mirror. Don't compare yourself to others. It only breeds envy and resentment. When you compete with yourself, you both win.

Count your blessings. Take inventory of the wonderful things in your life. Appreciate what you have, while you have it, or you'll learn what it meant to you — after you lose it.

Create good habits. Identify your bad habits and adjust your behavior accordingly. Remember, practice doesn't make perfect if you're doing it wrong.

Hit lots of singles. Strive for small wins. They offer confidence and momentum as you pursue your long-term goals.

Meet challenges head-on. Prove you can overcome tough obstacles. That will give you the strength and determination to face new ones. If you believe you can't, you won't.

Forgive yourself. Don't beat yourself up for mistakes or failures. Everyone is human — we prove that every day. Learn and move on.

Let grudges go. Seeking retaliation, rather than forgiveness, traps you in the anger. Let it go.

Avoid becoming dependent. Determine whether a "handout" helps you get back on your feet or enslaves you to a lifetime of dependency.

LIFE ISN'T PERFECT — STOP BEING A VICTIM

Life isn't easy. It's that simple. We *all* encounter problems, face obstacles, and experience setbacks. Why should it be any different for you? So stop the whining, blaming, and negativity. You're only hurting yourself.

Great athletes know that winning is as much mental as it is physical. Success takes effort day in and day out — even when your body says "enough." There is great truth to the saying that "what doesn't kill you makes you stronger." Overcoming setbacks will give you the confidence, strength, and determination to meet your next challenge. The opposite is also true. Being handed everything on a silver platter will cause atrophy of the soul. Don't make yourself a victim. Winners make the effort while losers make excuses. :)

SOME PEOPLE
ARE KINDER
TO STRANGERS
THAN THEY ARE
TO THEMSELVES.

BE NICE TO YOURSELF

How would you feel if someone put you down every minute of every day? It would be painful and exhausting, wouldn't it? What if you had to live with this person? Sounds unbearable, right? The fact is, some people are kinder to strangers than they are to themselves — they're negative, condescending, and outright cruel to themselves.

Are you nice to yourself?

15 EMOTIONALLY DESTRUCTIVE PHRASES

Do you have a tendency to criticize and belittle yourself? Is it so ingrained in your routine that you don't even recognize it anymore? Here are 15 things that you'd never say to someone else, but you may be saying to yourself:

You Said What?	Translation
"I'm such an idiot."	I'm stupid.
"I can't do anything right."	I'm incompetent.
"This could only happen to me."	I'm a mess.
"I'd rather keep to myself."	I'm unpopular.
"Why try?"	I'm unsuccessful.
"I'll never be as good as them."	I'm average.
"I'm so fat."	I'm unattractive.

"I may as well quit."	I'm a failure.
"I'm not asking for help."	I'm needy.
"My opinion doesn't matter."	I'm unimportant.
"Nothing ever goes my way."	I'm unlucky.
"I wish I could disappear."	I'm worthless.
"I don't really deserve it."	I'm unworthy.
"People like me never stand a chance."	I'm inferior.
"I'll never win."	I'm such a loser.

It's one thing to expect perfection of yourself, yet quite another to beat yourself up for coming up short. Choose your words carefully. You'll probably believe what you say.

SPEAK YOUR MIND, BUT BE NICE TO YOURSELF

Why would you say something to yourself that you wouldn't say to a good friend?

Break the bad habit. Be aware of every time that you're unkind to yourself. Create a catch phrase, such as "Be nice," to remind yourself to stop. It'll help to break the cycle.

Begin and end your day with kindness. After waking up and before you go to bed, tell yourself why you're special, areas in which you performed well, and things to be grateful for.

Give yourself a pep talk. Give yourself some encouragement when you're down or need an extra push.

Create a list of wins. Document how special you are. Include examples of when you:

Made someone feel special.
Went out of your way for a friend.
Performed better than expected.

Left your comfort zone.
Overcame an obstacle.
Pushed through a tough patch.
Helped someone in need.
Served as an exemplary role model.
Received a special compliment.

Although you do these things every day, you may be overlooking them. The sheer number of items on your list will give you reason to pause...smile... and feel good about yourself.

Celebrate small wins. Give yourself a pat on the back when you perform well. If you'd tell a colleague that they did a good job, there's no harm in saying the same to yourself.

Hold your head up high. Change your mood by changing your behavior. As Dale Carnegie said, "Act enthusiastic and you'll be enthusiastic." Before you know it, behavior becomes habit.

BE YOUR OWN BEST FRIEND

Saying is believing. Whenever you say something positive or negative about yourself, you look for evidence to support your claim. This can have a powerful effect on behavior and ultimately, on results. If you want to be beneficial, be positive. Stop criticizing, judging, or finding fault with yourself. You're only sabotaging your efforts. Instead, be upbeat, helpful, and encouraging. And most of all, believe in yourself. You deserve nothing less! Never say anything to yourself that you don't want to come true. You may cause it to happen! :)

"

KNOW WHAT MATTERS
MOST TO YOU AND
BE *UNWILLING* TO
COMPROMISE THOSE
PRIORITIES AT
ALMOST ANY PRICE.

— FRANK SONNENBERG

IF YOU DON'T TRY,
YOU FORFEIT THE
OPPORTUNITY.

ARE YOU LIVING A DREAM?

It's important to dream, to think BIG, and to reach for the stars. BUT, if you don't pursue your passion with gusto, you're wasting your time because your efforts won't amount to any more than false hope. If you truly want to achieve "liftoff," you have to get off the couch, make a commitment, and give it all you've got. The fact is, success won't be served to you on a silver platter. Dreams, unlike eggs, don't hatch by sitting on them.

During your journey, keep one thing in mind. Many people blame setbacks on factors beyond their control. In reality though, lack of success doesn't happen *to* us; it's caused *by* us. Here are nine roadblocks that can stop you dead in your tracks.

9 ROADBLOCKS TO SUCCESS

All talk. Some people talk a good game, but that's where it ends.

Laziness. Some folks want the rewards, but are unwilling to put in the hard work.

Fear. Some people are so afraid of failing that they fail to try.

Procrastination. Some folks list every excuse in the book why *now* isn't the time to start.

Poor advice. Some people allow their friends to discourage them from pursuing their dreams.

Indecision. Some folks are like a deer in headlights. They're unwilling to make the tough decisions needed to advance their cause.

Commitment. Some people are *not* willing to make the sacrifices required to succeed.

Perfection. Some folks demand perfection and can't proceed until it's attained — which means never.

Quitting. Some people give up without realizing that they were inches away from the finish line.

TURN YOUR DREAM INTO A REALITY

Here are four points to serve as guideposts for your journey:

Give it a try. Don't wake up one day and regret that you didn't pursue your dreams because you let fear get in your way. Remember, if you don't try, you forfeit the opportunity.

Don't just sit there, do something. Progress doesn't begin until you act. So don't talk about what you're going to do…do it.

Go all in. Few efforts succeed by dipping your toe in the water. Be prepared to take the plunge or don't waste your time. Remember, pursuing your dreams is a marathon, not a sprint. If you're not willing to make the commitment, don't complain about the outcome.

Attitude is everything. Your attitude can serve as a headwind or a wind at your back. Be positive, optimistic, and strong-minded. Once you make a decision, don't look back — make it work.

Don't let your dreams become an empty promise — to yourself. Success requires passion, optimism, and hard work. It also requires courage, sacrifice, and personal commitment. Remember...you're going to have good days and bad. But every step you take will bring you closer to your goal. You're going to face adversity, and your resolve will be tested. You may even wonder whether you're up to the challenge. But you're going to get through the tough days by remembering why you began your journey.

At the end of the day, your choice is clear: Are you ready to make the required commitment or would you rather forfeit your dreams? You'll know you're up to the challenge if you refuse to let anything get in your way. So tell me, if commitment is the fuel for your dreams — are you running on full or empty? :)

IF EVERYTHING'S
A PRIORITY,
THEN NOTHING'S
A PRIORITY.

CHANGE YOUR PRIORITIES, CHANGE YOUR LIFE

Many of us take each day as it comes and then seem surprised to find where life has taken us. Consider this: Do you prioritize the areas of your life and make decisions based on those priorities? Or do you go with the flow — and leave everything to chance?

During your journey through life, you'll be faced with numerous choices that may be in direct conflict with your priorities. For example, you may be offered a fantastic promotion, requiring *excessive* travel that separates you from your loved ones. If your priorities aren't top of mind, you may choose to accept it — even though family time means everything to you.

The key, therefore, is to know what matters most to you and be *unwilling* to compromise those priorities at almost any price. As Yogi Berra said, "If you don't know where you are going, you might wind up someplace else." The fact is, change your priorities, change your life.

ARE YOUR PRIORITIES IN ORDER?

You may be thinking, while this seems logical, why don't people take the time to identify their top priorities and make decisions based on them? The answer is clear. First, some people don't know where to begin — so they don't start. Other folks don't want to make a mistake — so they don't try.

Last, some people are so afraid of making a decision that lasts forever, they take the path of least resistance — and do nothing. In all these cases, they get swept away in the currents of life.

Priorities serve as a guiding star to keep you on course. Every action that you take and every decision that you make will put you one step closer or one step farther away from your goals. Here are 11 guideposts to keep in mind:

Take the time to set your priorities — it won't happen by itself.

Keep the process simple. Select priorities based on sound reason rather than a complicated formula.

Think beyond today. Ensure that your priorities withstand the test of time. Although priorities should be written in ink rather than erasable pencil, remember that they can be changed at any time.

Make the hard choices. Determine what matters *most* to you. If everything's a priority, then nothing's a priority.

Invest your resources wisely. Resources are finite. When you overcommit your time or spread your resources too thin, you fail to dedicate the attention that your priorities deserve.

Maintain your focus. Accept the fact that you can't do everything well. Trying to be all things to all people leads to mediocrity.

Get ready to sacrifice. Choices have consequences. Saying "no" to one thing allows you to say "yes" to another.

Maintain balance. Happiness is not a matter of intensity but of balance. While this may sound simple, it's not easy.

Make joint decisions. Discuss your goals with your loved ones. If priorities are aligned, you won't work at cross-purposes.

Learn to say "no." Remember that subtracting from your list of priorities is as important as adding to it.

Get a reality check. Give yourself a periodic check-up to ensure that you're on course.

TAKE THE RIGHT COURSE OF ACTION

It's so easy to lose sight of our priorities and to veer off course in life. We let trivia overwhelm us, permit distractions to sidetrack us, and accept other people's priorities as our own. In addition, we run on automatic pilot without really thinking about where life is taking us. Before you know it, a day turns into a week; a week turns into a month; and a year turns into a lifetime. Before we can say "do-over," we open our eyes and wish we could live some of it over again. But unfortunately, there are no dress rehearsals in life. If you want to wind up at the right destination, you must know where you're heading from the start. Make it a priority! :)

MAKE YOUR
PRIORITIES
A PRIORITY.

TAKE CHARGE
OF YOUR LIFE

Are you the captain of your life, or do you allow others to chart your course? Many of us seek approval from others, follow the crowd, or try to keep up with the Joneses. This isn't a call to disregard your need to fit in or to reject the support of others. But if you're letting others control your agenda, you may be putting *their* preferences ahead of your *own*.

It's important to make your priorities a priority. While you may think that you're in charge, take a moment to review this list and then come to your own conclusion.

IS YOUR LIFE OUT OF CONTROL?

Here are nine ways that we lose control:

Defer to our parents. When we're young, we listen to our parents. When we grow older, it's hard for some people to pull away.

Respect authority. We're taught to respect authority. It comes as no surprise that we sometimes let "authority" unduly influence us later in life.

Follow directions. Some people would rather be told what to do than take the time to think for themselves.

Ask permission. Some folks request permission to do things even though they have the freedom to choose for themselves.

Afraid to say "no." Some people get sucked into commitments because they're uncomfortable saying "no."

Conform to groupthink. Some folks change their opinions to bend to peer pressure.

Look for acceptance. Some people go to great lengths to win acceptance from others.

Join the bandwagon. Some folks follow the crowd simply because everybody's doing it.

Keep up with the Joneses. Some people do or buy things because they want to prove they're more successful than their neighbor.

TAKE CONTROL OF YOUR LIFE

Here are nine ways to take control of your life:

Be self-reliant. If you're too quick to ask for help, you're undermining your confidence. Before asking of others…do for yourself.

Know thyself. Form your own opinions, set your own priorities, and follow your dreams. What makes you think others know you better than *you* know yourself?

Find the right balance. If you focus too much on making others happy, you may end up sacrificing your own happiness.

Step out of your comfort zone. Build confidence in your decision-making ability by securing small wins; then progress to more-significant decisions.

Listen to your conscience. Don't blindly follow the crowd. If it doesn't feel right, just say "no."

Set the bar high. Make yourself proud rather than looking to others for acceptance. Always do your best, and you'll never regret the outcome.

Keep your ego in check. Be content with what you have rather than trying to keep up with the Joneses. When you compete against yourself, you both win.

Know what you know (and what you don't know). Seek guidance from others when matters lie outside your expertise. But don't accept their input blindly. Make sure the rationale is sound before accepting it.

Trust your gut. Listen to others, but trust yourself in the end.

GET IT UNDER CONTROL

Get real. When you constantly seek *approval*, you give more weight to another person's opinion than to your own. When you're hijacked by other people's *priorities*, you don't have time to tackle your own. And when you *follow the crowd* or *change your viewpoints* to fit in, you're not being true to yourself or your values.

Be the person who makes *you* proud. Follow *your* grandiose dreams. Reach for *your* highest goals. Do the things that excite *you* and give *you* the greatest pleasure. Most of all, live a life that gives *you* purpose. This isn't a journey for the faint of heart or for others to take for you. Accept ownership of *your* life rather than relinquishing that responsibility to others. Get it under control. You owe it to yourself. :)

HARD WORK
ISN'T A PUNISHMENT;
IT'S A GIFT.

HARD WORK IS GOOD
FOR YOUR SOUL

Work isn't just about getting a paycheck; hard work builds character, promotes dignity, and gives you control over your life. But some folks don't see it that way. As Sam Ewing, the professional baseball player, said, "Hard work spotlights the character of people: some turn up their sleeves, some turn up their noses, and some don't turn up at all."

Some people will do anything to get out of work. Examples range from those who say a job is "beneath them," to folks who want to start at the top without paying their dues. Some folks try to get by with sheer personality, while others dodge work by hiding in the corner and then stealing the credit. Additionally, some people request promotions or demand more pay, not because it's *earned*, but because they *want* it. In all these cases, the common denominator is the same — hard work is not part of the equation. What none of these folks realize is that hard work isn't a punishment; it's a gift.

THERE'S NO SUBSTITUTE FOR HARD WORK

On a fundamental basis, an entry-level job provides valuable lessons. It teaches us to show up on time, follow directions, work hard, and get along with others. Here are 12 life lessons that hard work offers:

Expectations. Set the bar high. If you accept mediocrity, you'll be mediocre.

Courage. Put fear aside. Set stretch goals and leave your comfort zone.

Discipline. Stay focused. Remain strong when days are tough.

Integrity. Build trust. Keep your promises. Live with honor.

Pride. Make yourself proud. Always give 110%. It's the extra 10% that everyone remembers.

Creativity. Don't accept the status quo. Be a problem-solver. Make things better.

Humility. Accept wins with grace and learn from your losses.

Determination. Stare adversity in the eye and stay the course when confronted with overwhelming challenges.

Flexibility. Even the best-laid plans go awry. Be flexible and remain open to new opportunities.

Teamwork. Be a team player. Your colleagues' success is your success.

Personal responsibility. Accept responsibility for your actions. The buck stops with you.

Make a difference. You were hired to add value, not to be a placeholder.

HARD WORK IS GOOD FOR YOUR WALLET AND YOUR SOUL

Hard work builds character, contributes to success, provides a living, and promotes happiness. The converse is also true. When people are rewarded *without making the effort*, it reduces confidence, promotes dependency, and robs individuals of their personal dignity. The fact is, when any part of the human body hasn't exercised properly, it will atrophy. The same is true of the spirit.

While work provides a living, it offers you so much more. Hard work provides a sense of purpose. People don't want a handout. They want to know that they've earned their success, which enables them to have control over their lives. They want to wake up each morning and be excited to get out of bed. They want stimulating work that keeps them on their toes and contributes to their personal and professional growth. This makes their days more rewarding and their experience more valuable. This doesn't happen when folks sit on their duff or have success handed to them on a silver platter. It happens when people know that they've earned their keep. You can achieve anything in life as long as you're willing to work hard and you put your mind to it. Are you up to the job? :)

IF YOU DON'T THINK
TALK IS CHEAP, WE
NEED TO HAVE A
HEART-TO-HEART
CONVERSATION.

BEING "ALL TALK" SPEAKS VOLUMES

Call it whatever you want: "All bark and no bite; All sizzle and no steak; All foam and no beer." The meaning's still the same — talk is cheap. The fact is, being all talk amounts to nothing more than hollow words.

While some people believe that saying something will make it come true, nothing can be further from the truth. Unfortunately, that doesn't stop people from behaving this way. They talk about dreams (but never act on them), make promises (but fail to keep them), and spew noble statements about what they stand for (but let's get real…actions speak louder than words). If you don't think talk is cheap, we need to have a heart-to-heart conversation.

BEING ALL TALK SPEAKS VOLUMES ABOUT YOU

Here are 10 examples which prove that talking a good game is as phony as a three-dollar bill:

Couch potato. It's easy to talk about what you're planning to do, but if you want things to happen, put up or shut up. Just sayin'.

Starting "bench warmer." It's easy to sip lattes and judge from the sidelines. But people who can — do. People who can't — criticize.

Person with promise. It's easy to make promises, but honorable people keep them. I promise.

Monday-morning quarterback. It's easy to predict the past, but everything is obvious in retrospect.

Procrastinator. It's easy to make a New Year's resolution, but promises are meaningless unless you keep them. Even those you make to yourself.

Dreamer. It's easy to have grandiose ambitions, but dreams, unlike eggs, don't hatch from sitting on them.

Role model (not). It's easy to say what you stand for, but if words aren't supported by actions, they're meaningless. Saying one thing, doing another doesn't cut it. Do as I do, not as I say.

Do-gooder. It's easy to volunteer others, but generous people don't just talk a good game: they raise their *own* hand as well.

Sorry person. It's easy to offer an apology, but words are meaningless unless you modify your behavior.

BIG talker. It's easy to boast about *past* achievements, but what have you accomplished *lately*?

LET'S TALK TURKEY

Big talkers are so good at talking a good game that they allow their words to become a substitute for action. They voice their intent, but rarely act.

They complain rather than get in the game. They promise everything and deliver nothing. These folks know that their promises require action at some point in the future. And they pray that tomorrow never comes — but it does. And that has trouble written all over it.

If you talk out of both sides of your mouth, your behavior's eventually going to catch up with you. At some point the bill will come due, and you'll be expected to deliver on your word. Sure…you can probably dance to your own tune for a while. But just like the game of musical chairs — you never know when the music will stop.

When that happens, you can talk till you're blue in the face, but people will see right through you. It'll destroy the trust, credibility, and respect that took you so long to build up. In fact, from that point forward, people will question everything you say. Worse yet, you may even begin to doubt yourself.

If you want to be taken seriously, remember not to confuse talking a good game with living up to your word. When you say something…mean it. Act on your intentions, keep your promises, and honor your commitments. Make your voice stand for something. And make sure that your vows carry the full weight of your integrity. Promise yourself that you'll live by these principles from this day forward. Do I have your word that you'll give this some thought? Good…now we're talking the same language! :)

YOU CAN'T
CONTROL THE
WEATHER, BUT
THAT DOESN'T STOP
SOME PEOPLE
FROM TRYING.

IT'S BEYOND
YOUR CONTROL

Face it…some things are beyond your control. Yet some folks don't always see it that way. For example: We *want* the sun to shine on our parade and we get upset when the weather doesn't comply with our wishes. We *expect* everything to go according to plan and get stressed when it doesn't turn out that way. We *ask* folks to change their behavior and then we're surprised when they refuse to change their ways. The fact is, you can't control the weather, but that doesn't stop some people from trying.

What areas of your life are beyond your control? Here are seven situations to serve as guideposts.

7 SITUATIONS BEYOND YOUR CONTROL

If you can't change things, accept them as they are. Consider, for example:

Miracles. Some folks want the sun to set at a different time. (Well, that's not going to happen.)

Certainty. Some people demand guarantees, even when there aren't any.

Status quo. Some folks dislike change and expect the world to stand still for them. (How's that working for you?)

Unforeseen events. Some people want everything to go according to plan. (Good luck with that.)

Human nature. Some folks try to force their will on others. (The reality is, people change when change is *their* choice.)

Perfection. Some people expect perfection and work hard to attain it. They get anxious if it eludes them.

History. Some folks can't let it go. They relive the past, hoping to change history.

ACCEPT UNCERTAINTY AND LEARN TO LIVE WITH IT

Can a kiss turn a frog into a prince? I hope you answered "no." It may also be time to end your fairytale thinking about controlling the uncontrollable. The truth is, once you close the chapter on that thinking, the more likely you'll be to accept reality for what it is — rather than for what you want it to be. Plus, you'll make life easier by setting reasonable expectations for yourself; you'll stop running down dead-end paths; and you may even "go with the flow" every once in a while. Most importantly, you'll give yourself a break when it's impossible to do anything else.

The areas in which you *do* have control are notable. They define who you are and what you represent. They guide your behavior and determine your ultimate destiny. Here are 16 such areas:

Moral character
Beliefs and values
Outlook

Priorities
Choices
Expectations
Actions
Effort
Attitude
Determination
Opinion
Thoughts
Desires
Confidence and self-respect
Aspirations
Personal responsibility

You can't control outside events, but you can control how you respond to them. Think about it! Having a realistic perspective will help you to be happier and more productive, and it will have a positive impact on your health and well-being. If control is an illusion, why are you worrying, getting stressed out, and wasting valuable time and energy when circumstances can't be changed? The reality is, if you can't change the outcome, move on to an area within your control. (The list above is a good place to start.)

The Serenity Prayer, authored by the American theologian Reinhold Niebuhr, places this issue in its proper perspective: "God, grant me the serenity to accept the things I cannot change, courage to change the things I can, and wisdom to know the difference."

Know the difference...if it's beyond your control, it's time to let go. :)

YOUR LIFE IS
DETERMINED BY
THE SUM OF
THE CHOICES
THAT YOU MAKE.

MAKE GOOD CHOICES

"What do you want to be when you grow up?" It's an age-old question that you're asked early in life. What you might fail to realize is how much power you have in determining your future and in making your dreams a reality. The fact is, everything you do, the achievements you realize, and the person you become can all be traced back to one thing... choice. Make your choices carefully — for they will become your destiny.

NOT ALL CHOICES ARE CREATED EQUAL

Next time you forget that you're the captain of your ship, think about the choices that you make every day and the impact they have on your life. For example, do you:

Surround yourself with positive role models or negative influencers?
Satisfy your needs or try to please everyone else?
Set high expectations or settle for mediocrity?
Keep your promises or break your commitments?
Crave instant gratification or invest in your future?
Grumble about things or work to make them better?
Live in the present or relive the past?
Listen to your conscience or fall victim to temptation?
Forgive and forget or harbor anger?
Accept personal responsibility or make excuses?

It's your choice: what to think, how to spend your time, who to be.

THE CHOICE IS YOURS

Making a choice requires more than selecting between option A or option B. Here are seven factors to consider:

You determine your fate. Some people let things happen; others make things happen. The choice is yours.

Choices are tradeoffs. By definition, a choice is an either-or decision. As such, every time you choose one direction, you're also choosing *not* to take an alternate path. In other words, saying "no" to one idea enables you to say "yes" to another.

Choices are influenced by your attitude. Your view of the world can significantly impact the choices that you make. The fact is, we are blinded by filters that distort our thinking process. Be aware of these filters and the impact they have on your decision making.

Choices are not equal. Do you put first things first or treat everything as a priority? If you treat everything on your plate equally, you won't have adequate time or resources to address the important things.

Choices don't have an expiration date. Choices are easy. The tough part is living with them. While some of your decisions have short-term consequences, others will shadow you for life. That's why it's important to achieve balance between your short-term desires and your long-term goals.

Choices have consequences. Some days you'll make good choices; other times you won't. That's life. It's important to accept responsibility for your decisions rather than shifting the blame to others. Accepting responsibility will instill humility, boost self-reliance, and emphasize the importance of making good choices.

Not to decide is to decide. If you don't take the bull by the horns, the decision will be made for you. Your choice.

YOUR LIFE IS DETERMINED BY THE SUM OF THE CHOICES THAT YOU MAKE

The future you get depends on the choices you make. Period. No one's going to force you to go to the gym, invest in your personal growth, or save for retirement. Additionally, you can choose to be an honest person, surround yourself with positive role models, and live a healthy lifestyle. Or you can choose an alternate path. The upshot is, you are bound by the consequences of your choices. It's your life; own it.

One of the choices that you make each day is determining how to spend your time. The truth is, we all have 24 hours each day. Do you spend your time on things that matter most to you, or do you squander it and lack enough time in the day? The fact is, you begin each morning with a blank canvas. It's your life. You choose what you make of it. Get the picture? :)

PRACTICE DOESN'T
MAKE PERFECT
IF YOU'RE DOING
IT WRONG.

WHAT DO YOUR HABITS SAY ABOUT YOU?

Habits are routine behaviors that are so ingrained in us that we repeat them on a regular basis. They include such things as our morning routine, gym schedule, and how we begin our workday. Even though most habits are performed without thinking, give this some thought: When was the last time you challenged your routines?

Do your habits serve as a positive tailwind or a damaging headwind? Do they make you more productive and efficient or make it harder for you to accomplish your goals? The fact is, practice doesn't make perfect if you're doing it wrong.

KICK THE BAD HABIT

The first step in modifying a behavior is recognizing the issue and having a willingness to change. Here are 40 habits that may be holding you back. Do you:

Take people and things for granted?
Allow yourself to get distracted by trivial things?
Fail to keep promises — to others and to yourself?
Talk a good game, but that's where it ends?
Allow jealousy, hatred, and revenge to consume you?
Speak before thinking?

Blame others for personal setbacks?
Overthink things to the point of the absurd?
Refuse to do more than is asked?
Check items off a to-do list rather than address priorities?
Keep score in relationships?
Surround yourself with toxic people?
Fail to keep problems in perspective?
Refuse to admit mistakes or say "I'm sorry"?
Offer advice without being asked?
Try to please others at the expense of your own needs?
Confuse being busy with making progress?
See everything as black or white?
Refuse to ask others for help?
Follow the crowd rather than think for yourself?
Refuse to leave your comfort zone?
Let your emotions get the best of you?
Fail to learn from your mistakes?
Put things off?
Demand perfection rather than settle for excellence?
Try to keep up with the Joneses?
Say "yes" when you really want to say "no"?
Refuse to let go of the past?
Lose patience at the drop of a hat?
Avoid difficult situations at all costs?
Wait till problems get out of hand before addressing them?

Refuse to delegate and let go?
Take on everyone's problems as your own?
Beat yourself up for mistakes?
Fail to balance work and play?
Overcommit yourself to the point of exhaustion?
Look down on others?
See the glass as half-empty?
Quit at the first sign of a problem?
Start everything; finish nothing?

MAKE IT A *GOOD* HABIT

The benefit of a habit is that it enables you to operate on autopilot — allowing you to focus on things that matter. The disadvantage is that your routines are so "out of sight, out of mind" that you might not notice whether a particular habit is helpful or damaging.

If you're a creature of habit, hit the pause button and think about your routines. We're so busy, keeping busy, that we forget the error of our ways. Frank Outlaw, late president of BI-LO Stores, said it well, "Watch your thoughts, they become words; watch your words, they become actions; watch your actions, they become habits; watch your habits, they become character; watch your character, for it becomes your destiny." Tomorrow, when you put on your shoes, make sure you have them on the right feet, and *more importantly*, make sure you're moving in the right direction. :)

IF THE GRASS IS
GREENER ON THE
OTHER SIDE OF THE
FENCE, CHANCES
ARE IT'S GETTING
BETTER CARE.

IS THE GRASS GREENER?

"How are you doing?" Simple question, right? There are at least two ways to answer. The first is to think of the ways that you're blessed and highlight some of them in your response. The second is to compare yourself to others.

We compare ourselves to others all the time. We compare ourselves to friends on social media, colleagues at the office, and even strangers at the gym. We rate our appearance, possessions, performance, and even our problems. In doing so, we rarely consider whether the person we're comparing to received a head start, whether genetics played a role, or whether we're even comparing apples to apples. The belief is, if you're doing better than others, that's good, and if you're doing worse, that's bad.

Is your satisfaction based on what you *have* or on what you *don't* have?

WHY YOU SHOULD STOP COMPARING YOURSELF TO OTHERS

Comparing yourself to others can leave you with several possible conclusions. From a positive perspective, benchmarking yourself against others may encourage you to become better. You might think, "If they can do it, so can I." From a negative viewpoint, you might become so obsessed with how *you* measure up that you try to keep up with the Joneses at any cost.

"If they have it, I want it too," you think. In addition, you might adopt a pessimistic and unrealistic view of the situation. "Life is unfair. Everyone has it better and easier than me," you may think. This could make you angry or jealous and cause you to stop trying.

In most cases, it is extremely counterproductive to compare yourself to others. As Theodore Roosevelt said, "Comparison is the thief of joy." Here are six reasons why:

Perfection is an illusion. We're often blind to the *real* challenges that people face. Although you might think someone doesn't have a care in the world, they might be like a duck — calm on the surface but paddling like mad under the water.

Comparisons are hardly ever fair. It's difficult to judge a running race if people begin at different starting lines. In fact, most of those boasting of hitting a home run were actually born on third base.

Comparison can turn into judgment. It is very easy for a well-intentioned comparison to turn into harsh judgment.

Beauty is subjective. Some things can't be quantified; beauty is in the eye of the beholder.

Some things can't be changed. You might want to be younger — good luck with that.

Comparison can turn friends into adversaries. Some things start out as a friendly competition, but end up with hurt feelings.

KEEP YOUR EYES ON YOUR OWN PAPER

In school, it was common for a teacher to pass out a test and say, "Keep your eyes on your own paper." There are two takeaways from that remark. First, cheating doesn't pay. Second, it doesn't matter how the person next to you answers the questions — think for yourself and come up with your own answers.

You were born with a unique set of fingerprints. In order to realize your true potential, it's important to be bold, live your *own* life, and accept responsibility for the choices that you make. According to Zen Shin, "A flower does not think of competing with the flower next to it. It just blooms."

In addition, keeping up with the Joneses is like chasing a rainbow. While it might look beautiful from a distance, it will always be beyond your grasp. By trying to keep up with the Joneses, we place artificial demands on ourselves that undermine our happiness. These demands force us to work harder and harder to cross a finish line that keeps moving.

If you appreciate what you have, you'll never want for more. So the next time you're tempted to compare yourself to others, don't waste your time. If the grass is greener on the other side of the fence, chances are it's getting better care. :)

MEDIOCRITY
IS A CHOICE.
I HOPE YOU CHOOSE
TO SAY 'NO!'

MEDIOCRE BEHAVIOR IS A CHOICE

Nobody wants to be called mediocre. It's like the screeching sound of someone's nails on a blackboard. Yet, unfortunately, we're surrounded by mediocrity. The bad news is that it's contagious; the good news is that there's a cure.

Mediocrity isn't something that's forced upon us; we bring it on ourselves. The fact is, negative habits produce negative results. Mediocrity doesn't happen *to* us; it's created *by* us.

15 COMMON HABITS OF MEDIOCRE PEOPLE

Mediocrity rears its ugly head when people have a poor attitude, misguided philosophy, or bad habits. Know the warning signs and take appropriate action to counter them.

Lack of accountability. You always have a clever excuse or someone to blame so that you can dodge responsibility.

Complacency. You made it to the top and think you can rest on your laurels and live off your past accomplishments.

Victim mentality. You convince yourself that everyone's against you and that success is beyond your control — so you stop trying to affect the outcome.

Lack of candid feedback. You rarely receive, nor do you want, feedback, so it's hard for you to know where improvement is needed. As a result, you never learn from mistakes.

Low expectations. You set the bar so low for yourself that you're pleased with mediocre performance.

Poor reward system. You've stopped trying because there's no distinction in your organization between exceptional and poor performance.

Bad influence. You surround yourself with low achievers. Unfortunately, their behavior is contagious.

Lack of competition. You're the only game in town, so folks have no option but to do business with you.

No conscience. Politics takes precedence over doing what's right, and appearances become more important than outcome.

Get something for nothing. You're rewarded based on tenure rather than merit, so there's no incentive to keep up with the times or to go the extra mile.

Poor leadership. You *easily* achieve results because the bar was set artificially low. The truth is, when you tolerate mediocrity, you get more of it.

Lack of commitment. You dip your toe in the water because you're afraid to go all in. The result is that a superficial effort leads to superficial results.

Crave acceptance. You lower your personal standards to win social acceptance and become a member of the in-crowd.

Think you're a know-it-all. You put learning on the back burner and become obsolete over time.

Apathy. You've been underperforming for so long you don't even recognize excellence anymore.

ARE YOU IN DANGER OF BECOMING MEDIOCRE?

If you think mediocre behavior is acceptable, I have news for you. Just as exercise conditions your body and makes you stronger and more resilient, the same holds true for your mindset. When there are no consequences for mediocre behavior, you can easily be lulled into a false sense of security — believing that mediocrity doesn't matter.

The problem is, when you think you're fooling the world, you're only kidding yourself.

One day, when it's important for you to put your best foot forward, you'll learn that your skills have atrophied and you've lost your edge. You'll come to realize that you've been coasting for so long that mediocrity isn't just a bad habit — it's who you are. Please don't let that happen!

Have you ever had a parent, coach, teacher, or boss who pushed you to your limits? The odds are that you resented them, and you may even have mumbled under your breath. The truth is, they gave you the gift of a lifetime. They helped mold you into a strong, confident, and productive person. They also taught you to demand a lot of yourself because you have the potential to achieve anything you desire — as long as you work hard and put your mind to it. The fact is, their gift will remain with you for life. It's in your DNA. They taught you to make yourself proud and never to succumb to mediocrity. The fact is, mediocre behavior is a choice. I hope you choose to say "NO!" :)

THERE'S A DIRECT
CORRELATION
BETWEEN
INTEGRITY
AND RESULTS.

DOES IT PAY TO BE ETHICAL?

If you asked people whether they'd prefer to work for an ethical company, 9 out of 10 people would say "Yes." If you asked the same folks whether they'd run their organization that way if they were in charge, they'd say "Absolutely!" BUT, what actually happens when they have the chance? Well…that's a different story.

They tell you it's one thing to be principled in theory, but it's another thing in the real world. Worse yet, they tell you they'd be operating at a real disadvantage if they ran their organization that way. What do you think? Does it pay to be ethical?

The fact is, there's a direct correlation between integrity and results. (That applies to every facet of life.) So where's the disconnect?

THERE ARE SIMPLY NO SHORTCUTS IN THE LONG RUN

When we're faced with a challenge, our first inclination is to take the easy route to address it. But in doing so, some people discount the impact of those actions in the long term. For example:

> From a *personal* perspective, some people step on others to get ahead, sell their soul to make a buck, take a lot yet only give a little, and make promises with no intention of keeping them.

From a *business* perspective, some people stretch the truth to get the sale, push employees past their limit to increase productivity, bully suppliers to win concessions, negotiate with partners to gain the upper hand, and focus on new customers at the expense of existing ones.

It doesn't matter whether you're under pressure to perform or trying to look like a superstar, achieving success through unethical behavior is a high price to pay. Of course, some people will tell you, "I'm only doing it this one time," but we know better. It's like an addiction that started out innocently and turned into dependence. Many of these folks are in denial — blind to the damage that their unethical behavior is causing them and their organization.

If you think unprincipled behavior won't come back to bite you one day, you've got it wrong! Organizations tainted by unethical behavior experience a higher level of mistrust, selfishness, and disloyalty. In addition, immoral behavior increases stress, irritability, and gamesmanship; people opt for political expediency rather than for doing what is right. It's no wonder that attracting and retaining exceptional people is more difficult — organizations that demonstrate unprincipled behavior have lousy reputations. Bottom line: Unethical behavior significantly increases the cost of doing business.

IT PAYS TO BE PRINCIPLED

Real leaders achieve balance between short-term performance and building a better future. They know that instilling a strong culture and promoting ethical core values are instrumental for success. Where do you begin, you ask? Do things for the right reasons and the money will follow. Whatever is in *their* best interest is in *your* best interest.

When you act with honor and integrity at all times, not just when it's convenient, you'll differentiate yourself and your organization from those who are looking out only for themselves or who are out to make a quick buck. This isn't achieved through smoke and mirrors, but rather through honorable behavior that's exhibited every day.

If you hire exceptional people, train them well, inspire them, and then get out of their way, they will produce outstanding results. If you treat suppliers as members of your own organization, create an environment where everybody wins, and build relationships based on honesty, trust, and respect, they will reward you with commitment and loyalty. If you view customers as long-term assets rather than an immediate sales transaction, and develop policies based on optimizing customer value, they will reward you with increased market share and profits. Last, but not least, giving back to the community not only makes an organization a good global citizen, it's incredibly good business. It is important to note, however, that if you're doing these things *primarily* to benefit your business, you may be missing the most important prize of all — knowing in your heart that you're doing the right thing. When you do right by people, the business eventually follows. And those who deceive people ultimately pay the price. It pays to be ethical. :)

ARE YOU
OPEN-MINDED?
IF NOT, LEAVE THE
DOOR OPEN TO IT.

THE BENEFITS OF BEING OPEN-MINDED

People say you should be open-minded — accepting of people from diverse backgrounds, listening without judging, and considering all sides of an issue. Even though that's sensible in theory, some folks find it difficult in practice. That's troubling because having an open mind is not only the right thing to do, it's beneficial in ways you've never imagined.

If being open-minded is so advantageous, why doesn't everyone embrace it? For some folks, being closed-minded is a *habit* — they're uninterested, misinformed, and dismissive of fresh viewpoints. Being closed-minded may also be the result of an entrenched mindset of *intolerance* or *prejudice*. Are you open-minded?

YOU MAY NOT BE AS OPEN-MINDED AS YOU THINK

Some people are so closed-minded that they can't see the forest OR the trees. Keep an open mind as you review this list.

Do you:

> Make up your mind before you start?
>
> Surround yourself *exclusively* with like-minded people?
>
> Discount or ignore opposing viewpoints?

Feel you're too old to learn anything new?

Make decisions without input?

Subscribe to a "we've always done it this way" mentality?

Spend more time talking than listening?

Use language or jargon that isolates you from others?

Request feedback from *only* a chosen few?

View the world as black or white?

Judge a person's ideas based on rank, age, gender, or race?

Create red tape or a bureaucratic jungle that limits feedback?

Feel threatened by smart or successful people?

Bully people to sway them to your opinion?

Subscribe primarily to information that confirms your existing beliefs?

Feel that your title entitles you to be right all the time?

Separate yourself from others by belonging to cliques?

Think this list doesn't apply to you?

If you cringed as you read these points, it's time to open your mind to the world around you. If you still remain doubtful, consider the benefits that being open-minded affords.

BEING OPEN-MINDED IS A NO-BRAINER

Open your eyes. There are many shades of color other than black and white. Being open-minded helps you to:

Expand your horizons. Challenge your thinking by embracing *differing viewpoints* rather than limiting debate to like-minded people.

Enhance your decision making. Evaluate your options from *every angle* rather than being predisposed to one way of looking at things.

Expand your relationships. Promote teamwork by being *respectful* of others' differences rather than being judgmental and intolerant.

Challenge the status quo. Advance positive change by encouraging *debate and buy-in* rather than leading by command and control.

Build trust. Encourage *fair and objective* decisions rather than subjecting the process to your personal bias.

Enrich your personal growth. Remain open-minded to personal *feedback* rather than repeating mistakes because you failed to learn from them.

Find the optimum solution. Generate *several good possibilities* to choose from rather than settling for the first right answer.

Obtain the truth. Search for the *truth* by listening to opposing arguments and letting others challenge your views and opinions.

KEEP AN OPEN MIND

Some people are so closed-minded that their behavior is not only ugly, it's destructive. They bully and ridicule others, hoping to convert them to their way of thinking. The truth is, everyone is entitled to an opinion. No one, however, is entitled to force their opinion on others. Doing so is the surest way to end not only a conversation but a relationship as well. That doesn't mean you have to compromise your principles, but it's important to respect the right of others to believe as they see fit.

Open your eyes to the world around you. You just may learn something. It will make your decisions better, your relationships stronger, and it will transform you into a more enlightened person. Being open-minded doesn't require a major investment of your time but rather, a fresh new way of thinking. It requires you to be a sponge — obtaining information from various sources, seeking input from people of diverse backgrounds and viewpoints, and evaluating that input based on its merits rather than on whether it conforms to your way of thinking. Are you open-minded? If not, leave the door open to it. :)

MARRIAGE, LIKE
INFINITY, OFFERS
NO LIMIT TO YOUR
HAPPINESS.

SECRETS OF A SUCCESSFUL MARRIAGE

Remember the first time you met your future spouse…your heart started pounding, your hands got sweaty, and you didn't wipe that silly grin off your face for days. In the weeks that followed, one thing led to another and before you knew it…wedding bells were on the horizon. The problem, according to author and famed salesman Zig Ziglar, is that "Many people spend more time in planning the wedding than they do in planning the marriage."

Like everything else, if you take your relationship for granted, cracks will appear like weeds sprouting through a perfect lawn. Marriage is a wonderful institution. Nurture it and you'll find that love doesn't have an expiration date.

INGREDIENTS OF A SUCCESSFUL MARRIAGE

The most important element of a happy marriage is choosing the right person. Here are 20 other ingredients:

Make your marriage your top priority. There are many things vying for your attention. Know what matters most to you and put your heart into it.

Agree on the BIG things. Shared *beliefs* and *values* form the heart of every successful relationship and can ultimately determine its success. The key is to understand your spouse's viewpoints and gain agreement on how to move forward together.

Nurture trust. Trust is the glue that binds successful relationships. Trust is built through a series of successful experiences. If each encounter is positive, the relationship will flourish.

Keep your promises. When you break a promise, no matter how small, you violate the bond of trust. Remember, trust takes a long time to develop, but it can be lost in the blink of an eye.

Have heart-to-heart talks. Say what's on your mind and in your heart. Be open, honest, and empathetic. If something is bothering you, don't let it fester. Speak your mind. And remember, don't just talk…communicate.

Put your spouse's needs ahead of your own. Care about your spouse's happiness as much, or more, than your own.

Offer your unconditional love. Accept your spouse for who he or she is, *not* for who you want him or her to be.

Give your spouse space. Cherish your time together, but give your spouse the freedom to have his or her space.

Meet in the middle. Seek compromise rather than forcing your views on your spouse. Remember, the relationship is *always* more important than the disagreement.

Be a good sport. Be your own person, but don't forget that you're part of a team. Complement each other's skills and grow in the same direction.

Handle disputes with grace. Debate issues without making them personal. Once words leave your mouth, they can't be taken back.

Never keep score. Marriage is not a competitive sport. It doesn't matter who contributes more at any given time. It evens itself out over time. (And if it doesn't, who cares?)

Park your ego at the door. The two greatest time-savers are saying "I don't know" and "I was wrong."

Be grateful. Show your appreciation. Never take your spouse for granted.

Live within your means. Finances are a key source of stress in a marriage. Be conscious of your spending habits. Focus on what you *need* rather than on what you *want*.

Keep the flame burning. Keep courting your spouse. Love, laugh, and create lasting memories.

Ride out tough times. In the course of life, you will face rough patches. A crisis doesn't have to breed hostility — it often brings couples closer together.

Live without regret. Think long and hard before you *do* anything that places your relationship in jeopardy.

Share and share alike. Life is more rewarding when you share your life with someone you love. That means changing your mindset from "me" to "we" and to "what's mine is now ours."

Show some respect. While trust, respect, and devotion may be invisible, you'll know that they're present. They form the foundation of every successful marriage.

MARRIAGE: PUT YOUR HEART INTO IT

Marriage requires commitment, but some people don't take that responsibility to heart. They fool themselves into thinking it's like getting a new roommate, pooling their finances together, or an excuse to have an extravagant party. While vows sound wonderful, your actions determine the fate of your marriage.

People who put their heart into their marriage reap one of the greatest treasures in life. You'll have a soul mate to share your hopes and your fears, your laughter and your tears, your joy and your sorrow. The fact is, the love of your life will make your highs higher and your lows much easier to bear. As Audrey Hepburn said, "The best thing to hold onto in life is each other." Marriage, like infinity, offers no limit to your happiness. :)

HAPPINESS IS
A RESULT OF
BALANCE RATHER
THAN INTENSITY.

ARE YOU BUSY BEYOND BELIEF?

Did you ever notice when you ask some folks how they're doing, they respond that they're really busy? I ask myself, "Is that good?" Are they suggesting that being busy shows how popular, in-demand, and successful they are? I guess their answer implies that the more frenzied they act, the better they're doing. Does that make any sense to you?

Think about it...we pack our day with commitments until we don't have a second to breathe. Then, when we're at the end of our rope and can't possibly do any more, we add one more commitment — as if we're trying to drive ourselves crazy. Of course, when the slightest thing goes wrong — which always happens — we get anxious and flip out. The house of cards collapses. Right? Rather than learn our lesson, we repeat the same mistake the next day. The truth is, we're so busy being busy that we fail to see the error of our ways.

ARE YOU BUSY TO A FAULT?

Of course, if we had time to think about it, we'd certainly notice the stress and anxiety that this behavior creates. But there are other shortcomings that may not be as apparent. Consider the following:

If you weren't so busy, you'd:

Enjoy the *moment* rather than worrying about your next commitment.

Organize activities in an efficient way rather than doing things haphazardly.

Spend *quality time* with folks rather than being physically present but mentally absent.

Determine the *best way* to do something rather than acting first — thinking later.

Build deep, *trusting relationships* rather than superficial ones.

Tackle *priorities* rather than addressing easy items on your to-do list.

Address the root cause of a *problem* rather than applying a band-aid solution.

Show *gratitude* rather than worrying about wasting precious seconds.

Do things right the first time rather than doing them over and over.

START DOING MORE BY DOING LESS

Looking for ways to calm your hectic lifestyle? Try these 30 ideas on for size:

Think before you do.

Say "no." (And don't feel guilty about it.)

Fight the BIG battles.

Ignore distractions.

Avoid the drama.

Ask for help.

Don't look back.

Never reinvent the wheel.

Learn from others.

Tell the truth.

Combine similar tasks.

Keep problems in perspective.

Leave work at work.

Appreciate what you have.

Say "I'm sorry."

Settle for excellence rather than perfection.

Find a shortcut.

Let it go.

Learn from mistakes — yours and others.

Plan for an emergency.

Be honest with yourself.

Prioritize.

Learn the meaning of *enough*.

Unsubscribe.

Know your limits.

Think ahead.

Delegate.

Remember…you're human.

Listen to your conscience.

Just relax.

DO YOU WEAR A FRANTIC LIFESTYLE AS A BADGE OF HONOR?

We're running, running, running. Did you ever stop…and ask yourself why? Is being really busy all that it's cracked up to be? Is living a frantic lifestyle making you more productive, helping you to establish stronger relationships, or improving your quality of life?

We should give up the notion that more is always better, quantity is always preferable to quality, and that being busy is always better than having some slack in your day. The truth is that squeezing one more thing into your day doesn't always make things better. In fact, it can actually make things worse. Do you spend more time looking at your watch than living in the moment? Slow down. Relax. Take some time to think. You may find that's just what the doctor ordered. Happiness is a result of balance rather than intensity. :)

IT'S SO EASY TO
LOSE SIGHT OF THE
THINGS THAT YOU
CAN'T SEE.

SOME OF LIFE'S GREATEST TREASURES ARE IMMEASURABLE

There is a tendency to cherish *material possessions* and undervalue things that can't be easily measured. For example, what's the value of having truly good friends — who will always be by your side? What's the value of a trustworthy partner who will always do right by you? What's the value of having an impeccable reputation — knowing that you'll always be admired?

The danger is, if we don't hold these treasures in high regard, we may ignore, neglect, or take them for granted. That's a steep price to pay.

WHAT DO YOU TREASURE?

It's so easy to lose sight of the things that you can't see. Here are nine examples that illustrate their importance:

Personal growth. Everything that you learn makes you more valuable to your existing employer — or attractive to your next one. That experience may be invisible to you, but it's worth a bundle.

Honor. When you live with honor, your word is taken at face value, your intentions are assumed honorable, and your handshake is as good as a contract. Priceless!

Trust. Trust makes relationships strong and effective. It increases security, reduces inhibitions and defensiveness, and frees people to share their feelings and dreams. Trust takes a long time to develop but can be lost in the blink of an eye.

Dignity. What's more important than being able to look in the mirror and like what you see? (You have to live with yourself for the rest of your life.)

Reputation. Although you can't be in two places at the same time, your reputation serves as your stand-in whenever you're not around. (Make sure it reflects well on you.)

Respect. It doesn't matter whether you're young or old, rich or poor, work on the top floor or down in the basement. You can't demand respect. You can't buy it. And you certainly can't take shortcuts to get it. Everyone deserves to be treated with kindness. Respect, however, is earned!

These treasures aren't limited to our personal life. Here are a few business examples:

Customer loyalty. How much time do you spend chasing new customers versus keeping existing ones happy? Loyalty is important because it's much more cost-effective to retain an existing customer than to replace that customer with a new one.

Passionate employees. How committed are your employees to your organization? You won't find that information in an annual report, but it's vitally important.

Institutional knowledge. Whenever an employee leaves an organization, they take a wealth of knowledge with them. What are you doing to capture that vital information before you lose it for good?

SEEING IS BELIEVING

Still unconvinced? The moral of this article reminds me of the courtroom scene in the classic movie *Miracle on 34th Street*. The judge delivers this eloquent soliloquy rationalizing why we should believe in Santa Claus. Upon receiving a Christmas card containing a dollar bill, he says: "Upon inspection of the article [dollar bill], you will see the words: 'In God We Trust.'...The Federal Government puts its trust in God. It does so on faith and faith alone. It's the will of the people that guides the government, and it is and was their collective faith in a greater being that gave and gives cause to the inscription on this bill. Now if the government of the United States can issue its currency bearing a declaration of trust in God without demanding physical evidence...of a greater being, then the state of New York by a similar demonstration...can accept and acknowledge that Santa Claus does exist and he exists in the person of Kris Kringle. (Cheering!) Case dismissed."

God...Trust...Santa Claus? Have faith. Even though seeing is believing, some of life's greatest treasures are immeasurable. :)

"

IS STRESS INFLICTED
ON YOU — OR
CREATED *BY YOU*?

STRESSED OUT? YOU MAY BE DOING IT TO YOURSELF

O n an average day, do you control your agenda, or do unplanned events control you? Are things manageable, or do you constantly feel under the gun? Do you manage the daily pressure well, or do you feel as though you carry the weight of the world on your shoulders? Stressed out? What's the cause?

Stress and anxiety have a detrimental impact on your health, your relationships, and the quality of your life. Unforeseen events and external forces beyond our control create some of the stresses that we experience every day; other times we're simply doing it to ourselves. Is stress inflicted *on you* — or created *by you*?

STRESSED OUT? WHERE DOES IT ORIGINATE?

Next time you feel a knot in your shoulders or a nagging feeling in the pit of your stomach, determine whether one of these 25 situations is causing you to be stressed out:

Wait until the last minute? Some people get an adrenaline rush from doing everything at the last minute.

Bite off more than you can chew? Some folks view an overflowing plate as a badge of honor. It's also a constant source of pressure.

Refuse to ask for help? Some people are too proud to request assistance. They'd rather pull their hair out for hours than ask for help.

Set unrealistic goals? Some folks set unreasonable goals without considering the consequences — they'll have to honor those commitments.

Push your limits? Some people don't recognize their threshold for pain. They drive themselves to the brink…and then push themselves a little more.

Impose your will? Some folks try to change people who don't want to change.

Take everything personally? Some people get defensive when receiving negative comments. They view feedback as a personal attack rather than as constructive advice.

Control the uncontrollable? Some folks accept responsibility for things beyond their control, even though they can't affect the outcome.

Get down on yourself? Some people demand perfection and beat themselves up if they achieve anything less.

Try to be right all the time? Some folks try to win every encounter, regardless of whether it's important or trivial.

Allow negativity to consume your thoughts? Some people allow negative thoughts such as hate, envy, or revenge to consume them.

Try to squeeze 25 hours into a 24-hour day? Some folks are always on the run. They're anxious because they're always a few minutes behind schedule.

Refuse to say "no"? Some people get sucked into commitments because they're uncomfortable saying "no."

Allow yourself to be distracted? Some folks get so hijacked by other people's priorities that they don't have time to tackle their own.

Keep up with the Joneses? Some people measure success by comparing themselves to others. It's a never-ending game.

Fail to delegate? Some folks are control freaks and can't let things go. They try to do everything themselves.

Demand instant results? Some people lack patience. They want everything right away.

Try to complete everything? Some folks try to clean their plate before leaving at night. That adds additional stress to a pressure-packed day.

Pretend to be someone other than yourself? Some people create a facade to win acceptance from others.

Put out fires? Some folks take on so much that they do everything half-heartedly. This causes them to run from problem to problem.

Live up to everyone's expectations? Some people focus so much on making others happy that they end up sacrificing their own happiness.

Try to be macho? Some folks push, push, push. They refuse to take a break or give themselves any relief.

Demand perfection rather than excellence? Some people expect perfection and work hard to attain it. They get anxious if it eludes them.

Play catch-up? Some folks waste time and then pressure themselves to make up for it.

Ignore your conscience? Some people behave inappropriately and are then forced to defend — or rebuild — their reputation.

If any of these situations sound familiar, ask yourself whether it's better to change your ways or to bear the pain. The next lesson contains 30 powerful tips to reduce stress in your life. :)

IF YOU PUT ALL
YOUR EGGS IN
ONE BASKET,
ANY FALL WILL BE
A MESSY ONE.

30 POWERFUL TIPS TO REDUCE STRESS IN YOUR LIFE

We live in a stressful world, bombarded by increasing demands, added responsibilities, and by choices between our professional and personal commitments. Sound familiar?

30 WAYS TO REDUCE STRESS

Make every moment matter. Time is your most valuable asset. Invest it wisely or you'll be forced to make up for lost time.

Live within your means. Debt is a significant source of stress. Ask yourself whether buying something new, on credit, is worth the added pressure.

Build in "wiggle room." Nothing ever goes as planned. When planning life's journey, always have an alternate route.

Know your limits. Cut yourself some slack. You can't be expected to *constantly* go full bore or perform well under *continual* pressure.

Get it right. Do things right the first time to avoid having to redo them later. Remember, problems are best addressed before they arise.

Be open to feedback. Learn from your mistakes. Lessons in life will be repeated until they are learned.

Be grateful. Don't take things for granted. Appreciate what you have or you'll be forced to learn what it meant to you after you lose it.

Take calculated risks. People who live on the edge never fear falling off. But remember, when you bet against the statistics, you'll eventually become one.

Keep things in perspective. Establish priorities. Spend your time where it matters most, or you may live to regret it.

Manage your expectations. Set stretch goals, but make sure they're realistic. Talking a good game doesn't put points on the board.

Reserve "me" time. Give yourself time to pause. It'll help you keep things in perspective and re-energize your batteries.

Say "no." If you focus too much on making others happy, you may end up sacrificing your own happiness.

Work hard AND work smart. Stop and think. Being busy isn't the same as being productive.

Think small. You don't always have to swing for the fence. The cumulative impact of doing small things in a consistent manner is huge.

Plan ahead. Some things come as a surprise; others shouldn't. Start saving for retirement beginning with your first paycheck.

Be early. Don't wait until the last minute. Instead, be a few minutes early. If a mishap occurs, you'll still be on time.

Go with the flow. Unforeseen events can be alarming and disruptive. But they're also a fact of life. Expect it. Prepare for it. Remain flexible.

Shoot for excellence. Strive for excellence, not perfection. Excellent is more than sufficient.

Protect your downside. Be optimistic, but safeguard yourself in case the opportunity doesn't pan out. If you put all your eggs in one basket, any fall will be a messy one.

See the invisible. It's so easy to lose sight of the things that you can't see. Trust takes a long time to develop but can be lost in the blink of an eye.

Learn this costly lesson. Cheaper isn't always less expensive. It's better to buy good quality up front than to replace inferior quality later.

Be realistic. Don't expect rainbows to fill the sky every day. Life is filled with "ups and downs," so make the most of the "in-betweens."

Find the right balance. Slow down. Happiness is a result of balance rather than intensity.

Set priorities. Is your plate overflowing? Saying "no" to one thing will enable you to say "yes" to another.

Save for a rainy day. Build a cushion in case unforeseen expenses strike — they usually do.

Do preventive maintenance. Take care of your things so that you avoid unnecessary fire drills.

Let it go. Keeping things bottled up inside yourself is stressful and anxiety provoking. Hate, envy, and revenge are destructive and unproductive.

Learn the meaning of enough. More isn't always better. Stop working harder and harder to cross a finish line that YOU keep moving.

Chill out. Don't take life so seriously. Most problems aren't life changing. In fact, you'll probably forget most of them within two months.

Listen to your conscience. Actions have consequences. Be prepared to accept them. Follow your conscience. Sleep well.

Instead of living life to the fullest, we're all living life on the edge — cramming as much as we can into a day and scrambling to get ahead at all costs. The truth is — you may not have the control to lengthen your life, but you can do much to deepen it. :)

A LIFE OF *HONOR*
OFFERS ABUNDANT
REWARDS; A LIFE
OF *DISHONOR*
COMES AT A VERY
STEEP PRICE.

DO YOU LISTEN TO YOUR CONSCIENCE?

I hear about people who lie, cheat, and steal, and I ask myself *why*? Are they so mediocre that they have to lie to make themselves look good? Are they so desperate that they have to cheat to get ahead? Are they so hopeless that they have to steal to satisfy their greed? Most of all…are they so shallow that their guilt doesn't haunt them every single night? Why don't they listen to their conscience?

Some folks think their poor behavior is acceptable. I'm here to tell you it's not. They're willing to turn a deaf ear to their wrongdoings. The truth is, when you think you're fooling the world, you're only kidding yourself. A life of *honor* offers abundant rewards; a life of *dishonor* comes at a very steep price. Your conscience should be your guiding force every day.

10 REASONS WHY PEOPLE IGNORE THEIR CONSCIENCE

Poor nurturing. When kids grow up, they hear their parent's guiding voice in their subconscious. When parents ignore that responsibility, their kids get the silent treatment.

Toxic peer pressure. There is a difference between right and wrong. Poor role models are terrible influences.

Instant gratification. Some folks take shortcuts — even dishonest ones — to secure rewards. They don't want to work hard to earn their success.

Impulsive behavior. Some folks act first, think later. (What are they thinking?)

No consequences. Some people gamble that they won't get caught.

Everybody does it. Some folks excuse bad behavior by thinking "Everybody does it."

Repeat offender. Some people "get away with murder," and think they can get away with it again.

Sense of entitlement. Some people want something so bad that they *take* it.

End justifies the means. Some folks believe immoral behavior is acceptable if it's done for the right reason. Wrong!

Lie to yourself. Some people tell themselves they'll only do it once. Okay…maybe twice.

WHY SHOULD YOU LISTEN TO YOUR CONSCIENCE?

Make yourself proud. You have one life to live. Set high standards. Remain true to your values. You have to live with yourself for the rest of your life.

Live without regrets. There is a difference between right and wrong. Period! Knowing what's right isn't as important as doing what's right.

You're a role model. People look up to you. They're learning by your behavior. Don't let them down. Teach them that integrity matters!

It's good business. Everything else being equal, talented people would rather work for — and customers would rather buy from — companies that do right by their people, customers, and communities.

Build a solid reputation. Your reputation is like a shadow, following you wherever you go. Protect it like it's the most valuable asset you own — because it is.

Get a good night's sleep. Listen to your conscience. Sleep well!

WAKE UP AND LISTEN TO YOUR CONSCIENCE

I'm probably not telling you anything you don't already know. But ask yourself: If it's so obvious, why don't people listen to their conscience?

I'm not asking you to be a saint, but let's get real. You have one life to live. And YOU get to choose the path you'll take. You can take the high ground and live your life with honor and integrity. Or, you can take the low road and sell your soul to the highest bidder. At the end of the day, when you're lying awake at night, you will know which path you've chosen. I hope you chose well. As Robert Frost said, in *The Road Not Taken*, "Two roads diverged in a wood, and I — I took the one less traveled by, and that has made all the difference."

Care not only about where life is taking you, but about how you're getting there as well. Don't listen to me; listen to your conscience. :)

SURROUND
YOURSELF WITH
POSITIVE PEOPLE;
THEIR ENERGY
IS CONTAGIOUS.

SURROUND YOURSELF WITH TOP-NOTCH PEOPLE

A lot has been said about the impact that toxic waste has on the environment. Consider the impact that toxic people have on your life. The fact is, people influence you every day. Do they inspire you or sap your energy? Do they serve as positive role models or negative influences? Do they want what's best for you, or are they out for themselves? You probably know those who serve as positive or negative influences in your life. Surround yourself with top-notch people. It makes a huge difference.

16 TYPES OF TOXIC PEOPLE

Toxic people pollute your attitude, retard your drive, and corrupt your morality. They drag you down, wear you out, and bring out the worst in you. This doesn't mean toxic people always display detrimental behavior, but they definitely serve as a negative force in your life. As Ben Franklin said, "When you lie down with dogs, you get up with fleas."

Here are 16 types of toxic people. Have you seen any of them lately?

Critical. Some folks rarely see the good in the world. They find fault with everything.

Complainers. Some people whine all day long. Tiresome, isn't it?

Unethical. Some folks probably know the difference between right and wrong, but you'd never know it.

Jealous. Some people envy the achievements of others. They view success with disdain — regardless of the effort and sacrifice required to achieve it.

Backstabbers. Some folks say they're friends. Well…they're not.

Takers. Some people are always on the take. They're always asking for a favor. If *you* make a request, they magically disappear.

Pessimists. Some folks never see a bright sunny day. They only see clouds in the sky — depressing.

Bullies. Some people torment and intimidate others to make themselves feel powerful.

Haters. Some folks think they've been unfairly treated — they're angry at the world — and they let you know it.

Mean-spirited. Some people are cruel and demeaning. They treat others like dirt.

Hypocrites. Some folks are quick to volunteer someone else, but rarely (if ever) raise their own hand — selfish.

Moody. Some people have more ups and downs than an elevator.

Righteous. Some folks constantly work at persuading you to adopt their values or way of thinking.

Egotists. Some people have real attitude. They think the world revolves around them and that they're better than everyone else.

Rude. Some folks never learned proper manners. They're vulgar, disrespectful, and flat-out offensive at times.

Greedy. Some people never have enough. They're like sharks that spend their entire life hunting and consuming.

When you surround yourself with toxic people, you're forced to swim against the tide.

YOU'RE ONLY AS GOOD AS THE COMPANY YOU KEEP

Top-notch people contribute to your life in meaningful ways, as:

Friends. These folks make every day special. They care about you and are genuinely happy for your success. You can count on them in good times AND bad.

Cheerleaders. These people energize you. They make you feel good about yourself and inspire you to be your best. Surround yourself with positive people; their energy is contagious.

Coaches. These folks challenge you to leave your comfort zone; they offer constructive feedback to better your game.

Trusted advisors. These people are good listeners. You can always count on them for sage advice. They're honest, objective, and trustworthy.

Teachers. These folks show you the ropes in a nonthreatening way.

Role models. These people have strong moral character and impeccable values. You hope their behavior rubs off on you — and it usually does.

All these people serve as a positive influence in your life. They're caring, giving, and supportive. They set high standards and live honorable lives. They'll inspire you to be your best and help you to reach your full potential. The fact is, you determine the people you spend your time with. Choose wisely. :)

DETERMINATION IS
HABIT FORMING;
SO IS QUITTING.

DO DIETS REALLY WORK?

Dieting is like learning to drive a car. You step on the gas one moment and hit the brakes the next — start, stop, start, stop. Even though you're moving forward — and sometimes that's questionable — the ride is jerky. The same is often true of diets.

Does this sound familiar? You announce you're going on a diet. For the next few days, you starve yourself and complain bitterly that you're reaching your wits' end. A few days go by…you're so proud of what you've accomplished that you reward yourself by cheating "one time." Of course, one time leads to another and before you can say "weak moment," you're back to your old ways. This principle often applies to modifying other habits* as well: enthusiasm one day — abandonment the next.

The point is that quick fixes aren't as effective as lifestyle changes.

WHY DO DIETS FAIL?

If your diet didn't work last time, what makes you think it'll work now? Before you step on the gas again, what did you learn from your last attempt? Here are six reasons why diets (and efforts to break other bad habits) fail:

Wishes are just words. Hope without effort is destined to fail. Spend less time thinking and talking and more time doing.

Don't believe in fairytale solutions. Don't search for quick-fix answers. A band-aid approach is often a short-lived solution.

Personal responsibility can't be delegated. It can't be done *for* you. It must be done *by* you. There's no substitute for desire, hard work, and commitment.

Punishment is not a motivator. If you find yourself thinking, "I can't wait till this is over," you're heading down the wrong path. Don't worry if you go off the bandwagon once in a while. One dessert won't change mankind. But if you make the process fun (or at least bearable), you'll return to your effort.

An immediate result isn't a realistic aspiration. Be realistic in setting goals and committing to make change a reality. Be patient. It's a marathon, not a sprint. View your effort as a lifestyle change rather than a temporary fix. If you enthusiastically push forward, it'll become habit over time. The truth is, incremental progress leads to long-lasting results.

You can't live an unhealthy lifestyle and expect a healthy outcome. Some people expect results without sacrifice. Wrong! If you don't embrace change, don't expect a different outcome.

SUCCESS REQUIRES COMMITMENT

There are three lessons that can be learned from diets that fail:

When you make promises to yourself, keep them. If the effort is important to you, see it through to fruition. Or don't do it at all.

Determination is habit forming; so is quitting. When you surrender to weaknesses, you're letting yourself down. Every time you quit, you make it easier to tell yourself that quitting is acceptable. That's detrimental to all your future efforts. Conversely, every time you show determination, you build inner strength to overcome other challenges that you'll face in the future.

Willpower is nothing more than desire. You have the power to achieve anything you want as long as you work hard and have the determination to succeed. Believe in yourself. Don't outsource your responsibility or expect others to do the heavy lifting. You have to make it happen. Enjoy the process. Don't view the effort as a chore. The truth is, although incremental progress won't produce instant results, little steps cover a lot of ground over time. Give it a try. It takes many years to become an overnight success. **:)**

*Some issues may require professional counsel. It's important to recognize those situations and seek professional support for them.

SAYING 'NO'
TO YOUR CHILDREN
CAN BE AN ACT
OF LOVE.

ARE YOU PREPARING YOUR KIDS FOR THE REAL WORLD?

We baby our kids like infants; we coddle them like delicate crystal; and we pamper them like they're totally incapable of surviving on their own. I can just hear the refrain, "Whatever you want, dear."

If our kids confront adversity, we clear a path for them. If they lose by a mile, we give them trophies for trying. And when they have trouble coping in the big bad world, it's never our error for overprotecting them or their fault for being helpless — we condemn the system instead. That way, there are no losers.

Are we doing our kids a favor by making their life *unrealistically* easy? Or are we making it impossible for them to succeed when they go out into the real world — and reality hits them right between the eyes?

What happens when our kids encounter a competitive showdown, struggle with a personal tragedy, or face a challenge with impossible odds? Will you tell his opponents to take it easy on him because he's fragile? Will you tell her teammates to pull a little harder because she needs a break? Will you tell his manager to promote him, not because he's the most deserving, but because it's his turn? Seriously! We fight their battles, protect them from meanies, and pretend they do no wrong — even when actions *should* have consequences. "What do they learn?" you ask. Nothing! What will they do when there's no one to grease the skids for them or to get them off the hook? These little darlings will be unable to cope. And there won't be anyone to protect, defend, or catch them before they fall. That has disaster written all over it.

TEACH YOUR CHILDREN "HOW TO FISH"

Are you preparing your kids for the real world? Here are 13 guideposts for your kids to follow through life:

Be self-reliant. Don't allow yourself to become overly dependent on others. It can't be done *for you*; it must be done *by you*.

Own your life. Make good choices and accept responsibility for your actions. Your life is determined by the sum of the choices that YOU make.

Face the facts. Every day isn't filled with rainbows. Be prepared to accept the good with the bad — even roses have thorns.

Establish realistic expectations. You *don't* get what you want; you get what you deserve. Period.

Get your hands dirty. You'll start at the bottom and remain there until you demonstrate you can handle more.

Learn a thing or two. Allow your mentor to guide, but *never* to perform, an activity for you. This will instill confidence and ensure that learning takes place.

Take it slow. Don't bite off more than you can chew at first. Build confidence and momentum through small wins.

Don't blame — learn. Make mistakes when the consequences are small. That way, you'll know exactly how to handle things when it matters most.

Don't baby yourself. Show some grit when you're confronted by challenges. Determination is habit forming; so is quitting.

Take one for the team. Work hard. You're expected to pull your own weight, not to weigh down the team.

Invest in yourself. Education and experience are precious. Everything you learn makes you more valuable, and the benefits will remain with you through life.

Accept "no" as a gift. People who *don't* indulge your every whim are teaching you "how to fish." They're giving you the gift of confidence, strength, and self-reliance.

Work hard; work smart. Nothing is accomplished without hard work, dedication, and commitment. It takes many years to become an overnight success.

PREPARING YOUR KIDS FOR THE REAL WORLD

If you want the best for your kids, give them a good education, instill good values, and set them free. It's not easy to let go of the reins because we don't want our kids to get hurt. But, if you're preparing your kids for the real world, saying "no" to your children can be an act of love. Sure…they'll hit some bumps along the way, but they'll grow confident and resilient over time and will be forever grateful for your loving gift. When they were young, many of their books ended with the phrase, "They lived happily ever after." I have a feeling that if you follow this formula, your story will have a happy ending, too. :)

IF YOU DON'T
PASS YOUR VALUES
ON TO YOUR KIDS,
SOMEONE ELSE
WILL.

15 WAYS TO PASS YOUR VALUES ON TO YOUR KIDS

When kids are young, they're totally dependent on their parents. But as they grow older, their peers and their surroundings exert a greater influence on them. How does that make you feel?

Are you comfortable with the impact that tough kids on the block, trash-talking athletes, or raunchy pop stars have on your kids? How about reality-TV celebrities, greedy business executives, or politicians masquerading as "role models"? Do you know how much time your kids spend listening to gangster rap, watching violent movies, or seeing obscene chats on social media? If you don't know, you'd better wake up. The fact is, if you don't pass your values on to your kids, someone else will.

HOW TO PASS YOUR VALUES ON TO YOUR KIDS

If you don't play an active role in raising your kids, you're leaving it all to chance. Here are 15 ways to pass your values on to your kids:

Prepare your child for life. Communicate the importance of character, values, and personal responsibility.

Stand for something. Share your beliefs and values in a consistent manner reinforced in many ways. Leave nothing to the imagination.

Encourage exemplary behavior. Inspire your kids to do their best *and* to be their best.

Set an example. Show, not tell. Be the person you want your kids to be. As Robert Fulghum, the author, said, "Don't worry that children never listen to you; worry that they are always watching you."

Manage expectations. Establish clear boundaries and encourage your kids to live within them.

Give responsibility. Give your kids the freedom to make their own choices — but teach them that with independence comes accountability.

Make yourself available. Be available, not just present. When kids are ready to talk, be there to listen. Gifts are not a substitute for caring.

Communicate more. Create an environment in which open and honest communication is encouraged. Remember, when kids grow up, they'll hear your voice in their subconscious.

Provide discipline. Be tough, but fair. Let your kids know when they step out of bounds. The fact is, saying nothing says everything.

Keep good company. Encourage your kids to surround themselves with positive people who possess strong moral character.

Monitor the media. Observe how your kids spend their free time and whether they're being positively/negatively influenced by others, including celebrities, music, TV, and social media.

Cultivate skills. Treat every experience as a learning opportunity in which feedback is welcomed, mistakes are tolerated, and failures are viewed as hurdles rather than as roadblocks.

Expose your kids to diversity. Teach your kids to be open-minded to others' viewpoints and beliefs.

Spend quality time. Make time to create fond memories and bond as a family.

Celebrate excellence. Recognize and reward your kids' exemplary behavior with praise coupled with added responsibility.

Great parenting role models are never too tired after work to spend quality time with their kids, never too busy with their own social life to give their kids the time of day, and they never outsource their "job" to others — rather they accept responsibility for raising their kids with sound values. The fact is, they sacrifice everything, and I mean everything, to raise good kids. *Of course, even great parenting doesn't guarantee that kids will grow up to become happy, productive, and well-adjusted adults — but the odds are clearly in your favor.*

Whether you like it or not, your kids will be influenced by others. So your choice is to play an active role in passing your values on to your kids — or roll the dice. The truth is, raising good kids doesn't happen by chance. Behind every good kid are parents or caregivers who understand the importance of raising them that way. :)

LESSONS IN LIFE
WILL BE
REPEATED
UNTIL THEY
ARE LEARNED.

LIFE LESSONS: THE IMPORTANCE OF STORYTELLING

Some experiences are so momentous that they have the potential to be life changing. My parents endured two of them. They passed valuable lessons on to us by recounting stories that molded our character, shaped our values, and influenced our outlook on life. Are you passing important lessons on to others?

My parents fled Germany during the Hitler regime with only the possessions they could carry. They didn't complain about what life dealt them because they knew they were lucky to make it safely to America. Like many others, they had hopes of building a life for their family and living the American Dream. The other event that had far-reaching consequences on my parents' generation was the Great Depression. Everyone alive at the time was deeply touched by that experience.

13 POWERFUL LIFE LESSONS

Here are 13 lessons that were passed down to us from those experiences:

Be present. Leave the past behind and enjoy each moment of today. Be flexible and adapt to change. You never know what the future holds.

Be self-reliant. Acquire the knowledge, skills, experience, and moral character to be self-sufficient. You'll depend on it one day.

Be resilient. There will be times when your determination will be tested. Be strong when the consequences are low. You'll need to garner that inner strength when the consequences are high.

Be tolerant. Be open-minded. You can't expect others to abandon their values any more than you would forsake our own.

Be frugal. Know the value of a dollar and make informed and thoughtful decisions. My parents told us, "Never leave a room with the lights on and always eat everything on your plate."

Be realistic. Don't get too attached to possessions. Material possessions get old and wear out. Memories last forever.

Be diligent. You can achieve your dreams as long as you're willing to work hard and put your mind to it. Part of your reward is in knowing that your success was earned through hard work and sacrifice.

Be your own person. Don't follow others blindly. Many people who jump on the bandwagon are uninformed or misinformed.

Be knowledgeable. Listen to both sides of a debate before forming your opinion. If someone tries to shut down discussion, ask yourself *why*.

Be heard. Speak up against injustice. Listen to your conscience and do what's right. Period. As Edmund Burke said, "The only thing necessary for the triumph of evil is for good men to do nothing."

Be selective. Measure a person's worth by their character, not their possessions.

Be grateful. We have the right to privacy, the freedom to speak our mind, and the privilege to practice the religion of our choice. People gave their lives to protect these liberties, so we should never take these freedoms for granted.

Be proud. A country is only as good as the makeup of its citizens. It is our duty to build on the promise of the American Dream and to leave a better world for our children. As John F. Kennedy said, "Ask not what your country can do for you, ask what you can do for your country."

LIFE LESSONS COME ALIVE THROUGH STORYTELLING

As leaders, role models, and parents, we must utilize every opportunity available to us to reinforce the values and beliefs that we hold dear. Once these values are adopted, they affect our day-to-day actions, determine what's important, and reinforce appropriate behavior.

There are several ways to achieve that end. They include showcasing heroes, observing rituals and ceremonies, honoring traditions, and telling stories. Storytelling is a powerful tool based on first-hand experience, told by a trusted source and delivered from the heart.

If we fail to promote the values that we hold dear, over time our beliefs will be so diluted that we'll open our eyes one day and won't recognize "our world" anymore. If we fail, the values that support the backbone of our country, family, and faith will have drifted for so long that the fabric of our society will be torn. It's up to you. If you don't pass your values on to your kids, someone else will. Lessons in life will be repeated until they are learned. :)

SURROUNDING
YOURSELF WITH
'YES' PEOPLE
IS LIKE TALKING
TO YOURSELF.

THIS DISCUSSION HAS NO ROOM FOR DEBATE

Why do leaders surround themselves with "yes" people? Why do managers reward employees for thinking alike? Why do people tune into news that validates their existing beliefs? These statements beg the obvious question: Why do people need to confirm their own thinking? And what do they lose by limiting discussion and debate?

Some folks seek conformity because it's easy and safe — they don't want any surprises. Others restrict debate in the interest of time; they opt for the first answer rather than the best one to address a pressing issue. Yet other people suppress information, limit discussion, and restrict debate for a devious reason — to retain power and control.

When you suppress information, limit discussion, or restrict debate, you stifle personal growth, impede innovation, and cripple progress. If you want someone to agree with you all the time, get a bobblehead.

ARE YOU UP FOR THIS DISCUSSION?

In order for **information** to be useful, it must be factual, truthful, and error-free. Information must also be comprehensive, objective, relevant, timely, functional, and credible.

Discussion enables people with different backgrounds and experiences to participate in a rich exchange of thought. They listen to one another, hear each opinion, understand the underlying rationale, and determine if they're in agreement. You'll never know if your ideas are sound until they are challenged.

Debate encourages people to challenge viewpoints in a safe and open environment. This back-and-forth exchange exposes the strengths and weaknesses of an argument and emboldens everyone to either build on its merits or discard it. It also facilitates the understanding of opposing viewpoints while it challenges everyone to consider various sides of an issue.

KNOWLEDGE IS THE LIFEBLOOD OF PROGRESS

How can you have a meaningful debate with people of similar backgrounds, experiences, and desires? How can you have a vigorous debate if participants lack objectivity and diversity of opinion? How can you come to meaningful conclusions if dissenting viewpoints are discouraged and frowned upon? The fact is, when you squelch discussion, silence opposing opinions, or shut off debate, conclusions are drawn from a limited perspective. Surrounding yourself with "yes" people is like talking to yourself.

If that's the case, why do executives lock themselves behind closed doors rather than soliciting input from employees, since employees are the ones closest to the customer? Why do politicians refuse to work across the aisle rather than seeking the best of both worlds? Why do universities bar those with divergent views from campus rather than facilitating the forum and letting students form their own opinions? And why do folks shout down, bully, and belittle those with whom they disagree — all in the name of progress? You don't win a debate by suppressing discussion; you win it with a better argument.

If you want to stimulate innovation, encourage bold fresh ideas, or solve the world's ills, it's vital to venture outside your comfort zone by embracing vigorous discussion and debate. It encourages wide participation, enhances clarity, and leads to more effective solutions. Plus, you'll discover that every new idea spawns additional ideas, which ultimately leads to progress. It's exciting, it's challenging, and it's productive. If you've been listening only to those who agree with you, I have news for you: People thought the earth was flat for many years. Go out and explore new horizons. :)

YOUR LIFE IS AS
COMPLICATED
AS YOU MAKE IT.

WHY MAKE YOUR LIFE COMPLICATED?

The shortest distance between two points is a straight line. The same can be said of performing any activity, tackling any issue, or making progress in general. Yet, some people opt for a topsy-turvy lifestyle in which everything goes in twists and turns. It should come as no surprise that this behavior can be a constant source of stress that can wreak havoc with your life. The truth is, it doesn't have to be that way. Your life is as complicated as you make it.

"Why do we allow this to happen?" you ask. Some people are unaware that they live this way, while others have bad habits that are hard to break. The fact is, many of us act before we think, live on the edge, overcommit ourselves, shoot from the hip, fail to learn from mistakes, step over a dime to save a penny, procrastinate until the last second, refuse to set priorities… and the list goes on. Then we say, "We need more time in the day," "We want more balance in life," and of course, "We're stressed out."

Do you go out of your way to complicate your life?

25 WAYS TO SIMPLIFY YOUR LIFE

Prioritize. Don't treat everything as being equally important. First things first.

Think ahead. Know where you're going before you try to get there.

Do it now. Do you procrastinate? Nothing happens until you start.

Find a shortcut. Determine whether it's been done or you'll reinvent the wheel.

Limit obligations. Free up your schedule. "No" should always be an option.

Learn by mistakes. Lessons will be repeated until they are learned.

Delegate. Get more done and buy more time for yourself as a bonus.

Pick your battles. Don't waste effort on things beyond your control.

Ignore distractions. Stop letting other people hijack your day.

Be your own person. Make yourself proud rather than seeking approval from others.

Be a problem solver. Address small problems before they become big ones.

Stop overthinking. Make a decision and don't look back.

Value relationships. Invest in relationships to avoid the time repairing them.

Let it go. Leave the past behind.

Plan for an emergency. Don't wait for a fire to locate the exits.

Ask for help. Know your limits. Never be too proud to learn.

End the drama. Gossip is a disease spread from mouth to mouth.

Add by subtracting. If something no longer serves a purpose, eliminate it.

Give it up. Don't impose your values on others. People change when change is their choice.

Live within your means. Learn the meaning of "enough."

Keep everything in perspective. Moderation is the balance of life.

Focus. Don't try to be good at everything — you'll end up being mediocre at everything.

Manage your expectations. Settle for excellence rather than perfection.

Be grateful. Appreciate what you have or you'll be forced to learn what it meant to you after you lose it.

Follow your conscience. You have to live with yourself for the rest of your life.

SIMPLE ISN'T ALWAYS EASY

"Life is really simple, but we insist on making it complicated." ~ Confucius

We've become so accustomed to making our life difficult that it's become a way of life. The fact is, misguided behaviors turn into bad habits and before you know it…oh well. Practice doesn't make perfect if you're doing it wrong.

Don't complain that your life is complicated — do something about it. All it takes is the will and the desire to make a change. Give it a try and you'll find that the effort pays dividends in ways you've never imagined. The truth is, you may not have the control to lengthen your life, but you can do much to deepen it. Is your life complicated? :)

JUST BECAUSE
YOU'RE AN EXPERT
IN ONE THING, THAT
DOESN'T MAKE
YOU AN EXPERT
IN EVERYTHING.

THE BEST ADVICE
YOU'LL EVER GET

How often does advice fail to pan out? Did you ever ask yourself *why?* Is it because we get it from the wrong people, misjudge the quality, or because we follow it blindly?

The problem is that we seek advice from the wrong people — some of whom don't have a clue about the subject; we follow the crowd even though we don't know many of them; we treat celebrity endorsements as gospel, even though they're getting paid to read a script. And still others seek advice for the wrong reasons — to dodge responsibility or to avoid the time-consuming task of figuring out an answer by themselves. Does that make any sense to you?

A FREE BIT OF ADVICE

Know what you know and what you don't know. Just because you're an expert in one thing, that doesn't make you an expert in everything. Seek input and advice when variables lie outside your comfort zone. Following are some guidelines worthy of your consideration.

Before seeking advice, know exactly what you need and identify the most qualified person to ask. I know that seems obvious, but some folks seek advice without forethought, while others seek advice from people based on convenience or proximity or ask the same people again and again — because it's easy.

Step 1. Know what you want. If you don't know what you're looking for, you'll never find it. Are you looking for:

Information. Are you fact gathering?

Counsel. Are you looking for an opinion?

Guidance. Are you looking for direction or help identifying available options?

Support. Are you looking for a sounding board?

Assistance. Are you looking for someone to lend a hand?

Recommendation. Are you looking for a reference?

Blessing. Are you looking for a reality check?

Instruction. Are you looking for how-to help?

Suggestions. Are you looking for ideas?

Step 2. Determine the key qualifications of an advisor.

My goal isn't to provide you with an exhaustive list of qualifications, but rather to demonstrate how an advisor's qualifications can impact the advice they give. Here are several qualifications to consider:

Subject-matter expert. Possesses in-depth knowledge of a specific area.

Trusted friend. Enjoys an intimate knowledge of you and your preferences.

Like-minded person. Shares similar beliefs and values.

Strong moral character. Possesses a strong need to do what's right.

Extensive experience. Knows the challenges and obstacles that you may face.

Objectivity. Views all sides of an issue in an unbiased manner.

Successful or unsuccessful track record. Knows what works, what doesn't.

Sound judgment. Offers keen insight and age-old wisdom.

Perspective. Plays devil's advocate. Possesses a viewpoint different from yours.

Similar demographic. Understands your situation firsthand.

Vested interest. Has skin in the game.

A WORD TO THE WISE

If you ask several people with different traits for advice, each one will offer guidance based on their unique perspective. For example, if you ask someone with subject-matter expertise, someone with knowledge of your preferences, and someone who is an objective third party, you'll receive advice from three vantage points. That'll give you three different ways to view your situation.

One of the biggest mistakes that people make is treating advice as gospel and following it blindly. Before acting on any recommendation, know the rationale. If it's sound, their advice may be sound. If not, it may be time to get a second opinion. It's also important that advice not be taken as all or nothing — feel free to cherry-pick good points.

Last, but not least, listen only to those you know and trust. There are many people who profess to be gurus or who are out to sell you a bill of goods. Take their advice with a grain of salt. In the end, it's never wise to seek advice merely to avoid making decisions yourself. It's your life to live. Own it! Make good choices. Remain true to your values. And accept responsibility for your behavior. Consider the advice of others, but trust yourself in the end. :)

WINNING DOESN'T
HAVE TO BE
AT SOMEONE'S
EXPENSE.

COMPROMISE: REDEFINING WINNING

Some people view compromise as a weakness. "Strong people don't compromise," they say. They're the kind of folks who declare their position, put a stake in the ground, and stand their ground at all cost. It doesn't matter whether it's business or personal. The outcome is still the same. What do they forfeit with this behavior?

If you define winning as getting the upper hand, backing your opponent into a corner, and winning at any expense, you've got it all wrong. You may win in the short term, but think about the relationship going forward. Do those actions build trust, teamwork, and respect? I think not. You've probably created enough animosity, distrust, and jealousy to last a lifetime. In other words, you may have won the battle, but lost the war. There's a better way…winning doesn't have to be at someone's expense.

COMPROMISE: A WIN-WIN STRATEGY

Some people need to win at all costs because their ego won't accept anything less. They'd rather win *personally* than accomplish something meaningful. Compromise isn't a synonym for surrender; it's a winning battle plan. Here are six principles to serve as guidelines:

Serve a higher purpose rather than bowing to self-interests. Marriage isn't a union of competing interests. In the same way, a relationship flourishes when people seek a common purpose greater than optimizing their individual position.

Identify common interests. Compromise flourishes when you promote win-win rather than win-lose, focus on what you *can* achieve rather than on what you can't, listen attentively to each other's needs rather than promoting your own, and show a strong willingness to serve the greater good rather than your own interests.

Focus on the relationship as much as the results. Relationships thrive when trust, teamwork, and respect form the bedrock of your dealings. The process can be compared to dating before marriage. Trust must be carefully constructed, vigorously nurtured, and constantly reinforced. Take the high ground in the relationship and do what's right. Be open and honest — closed-door meetings and backroom deals breed contempt. Demonstrate the true meaning of give-and-take through your actions rather than your words. Vigorously debate issues, but never attack someone personally or back them into a corner. Let them save face and preserve their dignity.

Ensure that actions lead to mutual gains. Relationships prosper when everyone benefits. Prepare to concede short-term wins to secure long-term gains. This is a marathon, not a sprint. Don't keep score — it breeds envy. Benefits don't have to be equal, but they should be fair. Be aware if benefits are shifting too much in *your* favor. If that occurs, find creative ways to even the score. The bottom line…never win at the expense of the relationship.

Focus on performance rather than petty politics. Relationships flourish when people are civil and respectful of each other's views. Discourage politics, gamesmanship, or any act that tarnishes the relationship. Remember: Opponents don't have to be enemies.

Compromise your position, but not your principles. There will be times when your conscience prohibits you from compromising. Present your case without grandstanding or demeaning someone who has an opposing view. Keep the disagreement between yourself and the other individual rather than going public. *Respectfully* agree to disagree.

IS COMPROMISE AN UGLY WORD?

Don't think every battle has winners and losers...many times there are just losers. A winner-take-all mentality not only impedes progress, it leads to gamesmanship, confrontation, and even resentment. Someone wins; someone loses. Long term, it's everyone's loss. That's a no-win strategy.

Compromise is a mindset, not an activity. It doesn't mean surrendering your values. The key is identifying common interests where everyone benefits. You build together and you win together. The fact is, you won't always get everything you want, but you'll always be moving in the right direction and building a trusting relationship in the process. There is an old adage that you can't win them all. In this case, you can. :)

PEOPLE WHO
RECEIVE A FREE
LUNCH END UP
PAYING THE PRICE.

IT MAY BE FREE, BUT YOU'LL PAY DEARLY

You were born with the potential for greatness. Don't let anyone take that away from you. The problem is, one day, when you least expect it, that potential may be snatched right out from under you. And you'll never see the blow coming. It will masquerade as a gift — a freebie — but it's the devil in disguise. The fact is, it may be free, but you'll pay dearly.

It's easy to be tempted by a freebie, but the cost you pay is real. Why pay your dues if rewards are served to you on a silver platter? Why shed blood, sweat, and tears if you can reap the benefits without putting in the hard work? While you may think you're getting a free ride, nothing can be further from the truth. Before you know it, dependency will strip you of your confidence, trample your dignity, and defeat your sense of purpose.

DEPENDENCY: HOOKED ON THE GOOD GRACES OF OTHERS

When you condition your body, you make it powerful. Every day you make the effort, you build strength; every time you overcome a challenge, you build determination; and every milestone that you cross builds confidence. The hard work and sacrifice make you better and stronger every day. Furthermore, when you cross the finish line, you can take pride knowing that you earned your success. The converse is also true.

Although everyone is born with the potential for greatness, freebies that lead to dependency can easily destroy that potential. When people receive a handout or have a silver spoon in their mouth, they are disincentivized from working hard, improving themselves, or becoming self-reliant. These freebies also lull them into a false sense of security and complacency. Before they can say "free lunch," their knowledge gets stale, their skills weaken, and their passion wanes. Additionally, they lose control of their destiny and become dependent on the kindness of others. The truth is, *every* effort should be made to help the downtrodden get back on their feet, but they shouldn't be absolved of their personal responsibility to secure a better future for themselves and their families.

Furthermore, when parents baby their kids by fighting their battles and shielding them from harm, they create a false sense of security, making their kids incapable of standing on their own two feet. The danger is, when pampered kids enter the real world they get hit with a ton of bricks.

THE GIFT OF SELF-RELIANCE

The next time you think about giving someone a free pass, don't do them any favors. While your intent may be good, well-intentioned behavior can have unintended consequences. When you serve someone life on a silver platter or make them totally dependent on you, you weaken their ability to function in the world. The fact is, people who receive a free lunch end up paying the price.

There's no easy road to success. It takes hard work, determination, and commitment. Don't let anyone convince you otherwise. If you really want to do someone a favor, give them a good education, instill strong values, inspire them, and then set them free. Everyone is born with the potential for greatness. Have faith by offering them one of the greatest gifts in life — self-reliance. :)

SMART PEOPLE
DO STUPID THINGS.
STUPID PEOPLE
DON'T LEARN
FROM THEM.

WHY LEARN
THE HARD WAY?

We all make mistakes. No one is perfect. But how many mistakes can be avoided? The truth is, some people repeat mistakes with alarming regularity. They make a mistake, get up from the fall, and run right back into the wall…again. Ouch! Does that make any sense to you?

Why don't we learn from our mistakes and then do our best to avoid them? Some people fail to learn because they have egos as big as the sky. Others are too busy, stubborn, angry, disappointed, embarrassed, or just plain lazy. Unfortunately, they learn the hard way.

Smart people do stupid things. Stupid people don't learn from them.

SOME FOLKS NEVER LEARN A LESSON

Ask yourself, "Do I have 20 years of experience or one year of experience repeated 20 times?" Here are 12 reasons why people learn the hard way. They say:

"I already know how it's done." Some folks think they know it all and don't have anything left to learn.

"I'll never be in this situation again." Some people think an activity won't occur again — even though it probably will.

"It won't matter anyway." Some folks think most failures are beyond their control — so learning from them is pointless.

"I don't have time." Some people are too busy to think about, much less learn from, their mistakes.

"I'm rarely wrong." Some folks believe they don't make mistakes. Obviously, they'll never learn.

"I always do it this way." Some people do things without much forethought. The last thing on their mind is applying lessons learned.

"What do they know?" Some folks avoid feedback like the plague. They believe that if they don't know about their flaws, they don't have any.

"No one ever told me." Some people live or work alone. They repeat mistakes because they're unaware of them.

"It looks good to me." Some folks have a weird sense of reality. Whenever they make mistakes, they convince themselves otherwise.

"I'm so unlucky." Some people believe a mistake is the result of bad luck. In that case, it's pointless to learn from it.

"I don't care how others did it." Some folks refuse to consider whether something's been done before — much less apply lessons learned.

"I'm too old to learn a new way." Some people think they've been "at this for so long" there's no need to learn. That's a mistake!

TREAT EVERY MISTAKE AS A LEARNING OPPORTUNITY

There are so many opportunities to learn from mistakes. Here are eight guidelines to consider:

Remind yourself that mistakes make you human. Making a mistake is acceptable. Just don't let it return for an encore.

Admit your mistakes and own them. Treat every mistake as a learning opportunity rather than a source of fear or embarrassment.

Welcome feedback. Treat feedback as a gift rather than a slap in the face.

Give yourself a grade. Life is a classroom. Every time you finish an activity, ask yourself, "If I had an opportunity to do this again, what would I do differently?"

Challenge your routines. Leave your comfort zone and be receptive to change. When people don't learn from mistakes, their mistakes often turn into bad habits.

Modify your habits. Ditch your bad habits. Practice doesn't make perfect if you're doing it wrong.

Think before you begin an activity. Determine whether you've done it in the past so you don't reinvent the wheel.

Learn from others. If you learn from the mistakes of others, you won't have to make every mistake yourself.

LIVE AND LEARN

Everything you do provides an opportunity to learn, but that doesn't happen magically. You have to make the effort to reflect on your experiences and summon the courage, desire, and commitment to apply the lessons. Although that's not easy, it's certainly better than repeating mistakes time and time again. Don't learn the hard way. Next time you make a mistake, throw away the bad experience, but save the lesson. :)

EVERYTHING
WORTHWHILE
IN LIFE REQUIRES
AN ELEMENT
OF SACRIFICE.

SACRIFICE FOR THE GREATER GOOD *AND* FOR YOUR OWN GOOD

Some people think they deserve all the good things in life simply because others have them. It never occurs to them that the folks they marvel at probably worked their butts off and made great sacrifices to earn those rewards. If you believe the American work ethic is "old school," you'd better repeat the class. Are you willing to make the sacrifice?

Don't get me wrong…it's understandable that everyone wants the comforts in life, but it's unreasonable to expect rewards without earning them. The fact is, rewards aren't there for the asking; they're given to the deserving.

You may be thinking this message is limited to material possessions, but that's not the case. The fact is, lasting friendships, successful business partnerships, well-adjusted children, and long-term marriages don't just happen. They're the result of hard work and commitment. Plus, you must be willing to make sacrifices if you want success in these areas.

ALL GREAT ACHIEVEMENTS REQUIRE SACRIFICE

Every relationship, romantic or otherwise, requires a certain level of sacrifice to achieve success. When you care for someone, you're willing to make these sacrifices because you have their best interest at heart, not because you have a gun to your head. This doesn't mean you have to forgo all *your* needs or abandon *your* principles, but relationships thrive when you forge mutual dependence in which you build something better together than you would have apart.

Friendship. There's a huge difference between a friend and an acquaintance. As a friendship develops, each person becomes more invested in the relationship. That means trust, respect, selflessness, and commitment become hallmarks. That doesn't just happen. It requires hard work, dedication, and sacrifice on everyone's part.

Business partnership. A true partnership is a win-win rather than a winner-take-all proposition. That means not trying to gain the upper hand, but rather, compromising and sacrificing for the good of the whole.

Marriage. Marriage is not a living arrangement or the pooling of finances; it represents the ultimate commitment. Marriage is a solemn promise to share your life with another person rather than going it alone. That means putting your heart into the relationship and embracing a mindset of "we" rather than "me" and of "what's mine is now ours."

Parenting. Having kids is not the same as being a parent. Behind every good kid are parents, or caregivers, who understand the importance of raising them that way. That means offering them your unconditional love and making the sacrifice that enables them to flourish and reach their true potential.

HOW GIVING ENRICHES YOU

Life is all about choices; you get to decide what you're willing to give up in order to gain the things that you cherish most. If you're not willing to sacrifice, you'll get what you deserve.

Some people think the world revolves around them… *their* comfort, *their* preferences, and *their* happiness. Although they want healthy relationships, they're not willing to make the effort or the sacrifice that's required. Instead, they're more likely to exploit every opportunity to get what they want… but at what cost?

If you want to build trust and earn the respect of others, you have to earn it. No one wants to be friends with or work alongside people who are egotistical or selfish. Good people make sacrifices for others. It's that simple. Be willing to make the first kind gesture and watch something magical happen. Whether it's for your neighbor, family, or country, people with strong moral character make sacrifices for the greater good. They give freely of themselves without any expectation of personal gain because they're as excited about the success of others as they are about their own. The way I see it, give of yourself because it's the right thing to do and more often than not, it comes back to you. Sacrifice for the greater good AND for your own good. :)

PEOPLE CAN'T HEAR
WHAT YOU *DON'T*
SAY. THINKING ISN'T
COMMUNICATING.

I'M NOT A MIND READER. ARE YOU?

"**P**ick a number between one and twenty-five. Wrong. Let's try again. What's my favorite color? Or my favorite food?" As crazy as this sounds, we bury our thoughts and then expect others to know what we're thinking.

Why does this happen? Some folks have trouble expressing their thoughts and feelings because they're shy, they fear a negative reaction, or they're afraid, after having been burned in the past. Others assume that if they voice their demands or concerns, they'll sound ungrateful or needy.

The fact is, just because thoughts may be swirling around in your head doesn't mean that others know what you're thinking. You can't get upset that people don't understand your needs and desires if you don't voice them. While they can guess and look for signals, they're not mind readers. People can't hear what you *don't* say. Thinking isn't communicating.

WHY ARE YOU KEEPING IT A SECRET?

Don't assume people can read your mind. If it's important to you, say something. You're not going to make things better by keeping it to yourself; chances are you may make things worse.

People like to feel appreciated; say something. If you take people for granted, you'll both live to regret it.

If an employee's doing an outstanding job, let them know.

If someone goes out of their way for you, say "thank you."

Don't let misunderstandings fester; say something. Problems don't get better with age. Address them in a proactive way.

If you think the relationship is one-sided, let them know.

If your friend just let you down, tell them.

If you don't understand why you were passed up for the promotion, ask why.

Don't let annoyances get bottled up inside you; say something. The alternative is letting them build into anger and resentment.

If the people behind you are being obnoxious, say something.

If your boyfriend's (or girlfriend's) habit is getting under your skin, speak up.

If someone continuously requests favors but volunteers little in return, tell them.

If your needs aren't being met, say something. People can't make things better if they're unaware of your feelings.

If you think your company isn't recognizing your contribution, let your manager know.

If you want greater commitment in your relationship, discuss it.

If you want more quality time together, say something.

Don't say you care, and think you're done; say something. It won't kill you to repeat your message.

If you love her, let her know how you feel, again.

If you're proud of your kids, tell them, again.

WHAT'S ON YOUR MIND?

Many problems arise, misunderstandings occur, and feelings are hurt simply because words are left unsaid. Do you internalize your feelings or express them? Do you voice your grievances or let them fester? Do you express your love and gratitude or assume it's understood? Do you voice your needs or hope others magically recognize them? The truth is, you can't read their minds, and they can't read yours.

Real communication requires more than small talk. It's important to build trusting relationships in which you share your thoughts and feelings in an open and honest manner. Stop talking to yourself and speak your mind. It'll enhance your relationships and save you a lot of heartache in the long run. As Napoleon Bonaparte said, "Ten people who speak make more noise than ten thousand who are silent." What's on your mind? :)

YOU WIN MORE
FRIENDS BY
GRANTING A FAVOR
THAN BY ASKING
FOR ONE.

HEY, CAN YOU DO ME A FAVOR?

People ask for favors all the time. So you'd think we'd have the process down to a science. Unfortunately, that's not the case. In fact, some of us are so bad at asking for a favor that we offend people, burn bridges, and even damage credibility in the process. Do you know how to ask for a favor?

Some etiquette is as basic as it gets. Waiting for the proper time, saying "please" and "thank you," and never taking someone's help for granted are a few examples of proper manners. Other forms of etiquette aren't as obvious.

AVOID 15 COMMON MISTAKES WHEN REQUESTING A FAVOR

There's a right way and a wrong way to ask for a favor. Don't be the person who:

Begs the question. Be careful how you request a favor. Begging may make the receiver feel obligated to help rather than satisfying your request willingly.

Behaves selfishly. Be patient. Don't jump out of the gate too fast. (When someone requests a favor just minutes after I meet them, I'm always tempted to say, "Dude, I don't even know you.")

Employs improper influence. Be conscious of your status. If you're in a position of authority (i.e., the boss), a modest appeal may be misinterpreted as a demand.

Beats around the bush. Be direct and clear. Don't take an hour to ask a five-second question.

Asks the impossible. Be reasonable. Never request a favor that's beyond someone's capabilities.

Makes it impossible to say "no." Give the receiver a way out rather than pinning them against the wall. When you say, "Can you give me a hand within the next few months?" — you make it difficult, if not impossible, to refuse your request.

Shames into submission. Select the right venue. Don't embarrass someone into obedience by making the request in front of others.

Guilts the receiver. Be straightforward. Don't minimize the task by saying "It won't take you any time at all."

Makes unethical requests. Determine whether your request is appropriate. If you're thinking about asking people to compromise their integrity, think again.

Returns for an encore. Be conscious of going to the same person again and again. That's taking advantage of someone's good nature.

Comes out of nowhere. Determine whether it's even reasonable to request the favor. If you haven't spoken to someone for a while, think twice before asking.

Resorts to bait-and-switch. Be open, honest, and sincere in requesting support. Avoid a hidden motive or trying to trick someone with a false promise.

Takes a rejection personally. Accept "no" for an answer. A rejection may be due to a variety of reasons, none of which have anything to do with you.

Asks for the world. Make sure your request matches the depth of your relationship. A marriage proposal on a first date is probably not a good idea.

Ducks responsibility. Before asking of others, do for yourself.

When *you* are asked for a favor, avoid these five common mistakes. Don't be the person who:

Keeps score. Give willingly without expectation of something in return. Your reward is the satisfaction of having helped someone.

Fakes it. If you're not the right person to satisfy a request, don't pretend that you are. Instead, suggest someone who may be in a position to help.

Breaks promises. Be candid. Don't say "yes" when you really want to say "no." It's better to decline someone's offer than to let them down.

Rubs it in their face. Be gracious by saying "You're welcome." Don't continuously boast about what you did.

Demands a quid pro quo. Don't ask for anything in return. Keeping score is a losing game.

DO YOURSELF A FAVOR

Real friends don't wait to be asked. They know their friends so well that it's easy to anticipate needs and respond before being asked. In fact, folks get more pleasure from doing something nice for another person than from gaining something for ourselves. Does this sound like you? You win more friends by granting a favor than by asking for one. :)

A SORRY APOLOGY
CAN ADD INSULT
TO INJURY.

NEVER SAY "I'M SORRY" UNLESS YOU MEAN IT

We all make mistakes. When you try to repair the damage, do you make the situation better or worse? We've all been raised to say "I'm sorry" after hurting someone through our words or actions, but is your apology disingenuous or a meaningful expression of regret? What are the ingredients of an effective apology?

An apology shouldn't be a knee-jerk reaction acknowledging that you hurt someone. An apology should be a statement of remorse with an explicit promise that it won't happen again. That means more than going through the motions of saying "I'm sorry" — your words must be authentic and coupled with a real desire to change.

A SORRY APOLOGY CAN ADD INSULT TO INJURY

If you can't make it better, don't make it worse. While people may be angry or disappointed by the offense, it pales in comparison to an insincere apology. Here are 11 common mistakes people make when they apologize:

Apology by text or email. Are you kidding? Make the effort to apologize in person, if at all possible. It helps to hear the tone of voice and read body language.

Forced into an apology. An apology should be a voluntary acknowledgment of responsibility. You shouldn't have to be coerced into making it.

Taking the easy way out. An apology should be heartfelt — not just an attempt to smooth ruffled feathers.

Hollow words. An apology should be a sincere expression of regret. But words are meaningless if they're not supported with action.

Face reality. An apology should fit the "crime." Saying "I'm sorry" may not be enough to make things right. You may have to go further to make amends.

Poor timing. An apology should be made as soon as the act occurs rather than letting too much time elapse.

Lack of commitment. An apology should represent a willingness and an obligation to make things right.

Recurring offense. Every effort should be made to repair and *not* repeat the offense. Otherwise, your apology is worthless.

Make excuses or rationalize behavior. When you offer an apology, be sincere. Don't say "I'm sorry, *but...*" You're either sorry or you're not.

Expect forgiveness. When you offer an apology, don't expect instant understanding and absolution. Be patient.

Quick fix. Saying "I'm sorry" is great, but that doesn't mean everything will be back to normal right away. The healing process may take some time.

HOW MUCH IS YOUR APOLOGY WORTH?

When you say "I'm sorry," you imply that you *notice*, you *care*, and most of all, you *promise* it won't happen again. As such, an apology is more than just a statement of contrition; you're putting your honor on the line. If you repeat the act again, you're indicating that you were more interested in creating peace than in changing your ways. You're also demonstrating that your promise isn't worth anything. If you care about preserving your relationship as well as your dignity, keep your word. If you don't, you will be forced to accept the consequences. As someone once said, "When you've done something wrong, admit it, and be sorry. No one in history has ever choked to death from swallowing his pride." Remember that words without action are meaningless. Never say "I'm sorry" unless you mean it. :)

"

HATE IS A CANCER
ON ONE'S SOUL.

PREJUDICE: "ALL" IS AN UGLY WORD

It's one thing to segment a group of people to sell toothpaste, but quite another to make a broad negative generalization and say it's true of all the people in a particular group. "All" is an ugly word. It's naked prejudice.

In the past few years, I've seen too many people assign labels to groups and call them derogatory names. They lump entire demographic groups together and belittle them, as if they all have the same fingerprints.

At first, when we hear these slurs, we view them as outrageous. But, over time, we become desensitized to the hate speech as the shock value wears off. What's worse, others begin to mimic this disgusting behavior. History shows that if hate speech isn't condemned, it can even become part of the norm.

I'll be the first to admit there's a bad apple in every bunch. But haters are quick to cast aspersions on large segments of the population, using a few rotten apples as justification. That's like throwing the whole town in jail because one person commits a crime.

Please don't misunderstand. If someone is guilty of wrongdoing, they should be held accountable for their actions. But that doesn't make *everyone* guilty.

6 WAYS TO COMBAT PREJUDICE
AND HATEFUL RHETORIC

Promote free speech. Free speech is the bedrock of freedom and is fundamental to our way of life. Free speech and debate are essential in our search for the truth. Therefore, we must expose those who discourage free speech, even if we disagree with the message in that speech. BUT...

Open your eyes. We should view hate speech for what it is — outrageous. People who condone this behavior or look the other way are part of the problem rather than part of the solution.

Remember, the end never justifies the means. There's no cause worthy of spewing hatred. Period. Leaders who pit groups against each other, for whatever reason, are unworthy of our support. Never judge someone you don't know.

Think twice before following someone off a cliff. Some people use hate speech to promote their personal agenda. It has been said that some protesters even get paid to make believe a cause has widespread support. (So much for *free* speech.)

Don't be a parrot. As Charlayne Hunter-Gault, the American journalist, said, "If people are informed, they will do the right thing. It's when they are not informed that they become hostages to prejudice." So listen to your conscience before sharing a hateful message on social media. Remember, some people hit with fists; others with words.

Promote your opinions with dignity and grace. Debate issues. Defend your beliefs. But don't demonize folks who do not agree with you. The truth is, people who disagree with you are no more stupid than you are in not agreeing with them.

PUT AN END TO HATRED, BIGOTRY, AND PREJUDICE

Standing up to prejudice isn't easy. If you're brave enough to call out these haters, you may be faced with retribution. Their allies may swarm all over you, like you're disturbing a hornet's nest. The fact is, bullies want to drive fear into your heart as a warning to never cross them.

You have to ask yourself: "What do we have to lose by not standing up to prejudice?" The answer is — everything! Do we want a world in which bullies intimidate anyone who doesn't share their opinion? Do we want a world in which angry mobs run through the streets with pitchforks? Do we want a world in which our kids could grow up mimicking this ugly behavior? (Remember, little footsteps in the sand follow larger ones, so watch where you step.)

It's time to reject labeling. It's time to put an end to hatred, bigotry, and prejudice. We can no longer close our eyes, or worse, become parrots to hateful rhetoric. Nothing good has ever come from demonizing entire groups of people. Hate is a cancer on one's soul. :)

MAKE A LIFE
WHILE YOU
MAKE A LIVING.

YOUR JOB DOESN'T
DEFINE YOU

One of my favorite interview questions is "Tell me about yourself." Some people jump right to their amazing career accomplishments, while others tell me about their passions, their purpose, or their family. The truth is, I'm not looking for a specific answer; I'm interested in knowing their priorities. What defines *you* as a person?

Some people think they'll wake up one morning and their path in life will be as clear as day. Other folks wait for the perfect time to determine what matters most, while others don't want to make a misstep. The problem is, if you don't identify what matters most to you, you'll never know if you're heading in the right direction or are off course.

If you don't *define* your priorities, you won't be conscious of them.
If you don't *commit* to your priorities, you won't achieve them.

WHAT DEFINES YOU AS A PERSON?

In many ways, life is like driving. Would you get into your car without a destination in mind? Probably not. As Yogi Berra said, "If you don't know where you are going, you'll end up someplace else." Consider these 15 questions:

Are you striving for success or happiness?

What are you willing to compromise to get what you want?

What could you eliminate to gain more time each day?

Is your goal self-satisfaction or acceptance from others?

What percentage of your time is spent doing things that you enjoy most?

Do you save money to consume or to buy peace of mind?

Do you do most things because you want to or because you have to?

What do you consider a higher priority — having more or being more?

Are you willing to make sacrifices, today, to secure a better future?

Do you let work demands interfere with your personal life?

How much influence do others have on your priorities?

Are you willing to forgo leisure time for money?

How often do you say "I should have," when you truly could have?

Do you value possessions more than relationships?

Do you pursue your goals or "go with the flow"?

STAY ON COURSE

Determine what's important to you or you'll *react* to situations rather than make *conscious* decisions based on sound reasoning. Here are six guidelines to consider:

Be your own person. Make *your* priorities a priority. If you focus too much on making others happy, you may end up sacrificing your own happiness.

Make the tough choices. If everything's a priority, then nothing is a priority.

Keep it simple. It's so easy to be blinded by ambition, power, and success. Enjoy the simple pleasures in your life.

Put your money where your mouth is. Learn how to say "no." Don't dilute your resources by investing your efforts in low-priority areas.

Keep your promises. It's easy to compromise your priorities, and say "It's just one time." Keep your promises to others — and when you make a promise to yourself, keep that, too.

Let your actions speak loud and clear. Make sure your actions are consistent with your priorities.

MAKE A LIFE WHILE YOU MAKE A LIVING

Too often, we get so caught up in the day-to-day minutiae that we lose sight of the big picture. And when we finally take time to catch our breath, we look back in retrospect and want a do-over for the bad choices that we've made. Unfortunately, there are no dress rehearsals in life.

One day you may reminisce about your life and ask yourself: "How did I do?" Here are clues to the answer: Did you follow your passion or try to please others? Did you focus on the things that matter most or just tackle your to-do list in random order? Were you grateful for what you had or was the grass always greener on the other side of the fence? Did you enrich *your* life or make a difference in the lives of *others*? If someone asks you to "tell me about yourself," what would *you* say? While career accomplishments are definitely *something*, they're certainly not *everything*. :)

EVEN THOUGH THE
WORLD IS LARGE,
ONE PERSON *CAN*
STILL MAKE
A WORLD OF
DIFFERENCE.

A TRAGEDY BRINGS OUT THE BEST, AND THE WORST, IN PEOPLE

Some tragedies, such as natural disasters, terror attacks, or even financial crises, are beyond our control. But we do have control over how we respond to them. Some people rise to the occasion and show what they're made of, while others... We learn what they're made of too. The truth is, tragedy brings out the best, and the worst, in people.

It never ceases to amaze me that some people capitalize on other people's misfortune. For example, some folks exploit tragedy to attract personal attention or to demonize their enemies before the facts are even known. Other people use tragedy to make money or to pit one group against another to further their personal or political agenda. And if that's not bad enough, some folks create scams to rob people before they've regained their footing. If you believe in karma, as I do, these folks are in deep trouble.

BUT, although there are devious, insensitive, and hateful people among us, there are also many unsung heroes who give of themselves in unimaginable ways. We should learn from *them* and emulate *their* behavior.

11 VALUABLE LESSONS BORN FROM TRAGEDY

Just as a rainbow after a shower, some behavior is a beautiful sight to behold on the heels of a tragedy. Here are 11 lessons that you can learn from exceptional role models:

Be smart. Problems are best addressed before they arise.

Be courageous. Run toward the problem rather than away from it.

Be action-oriented. Complaining isn't a substitute for action. Nothing happens until you make it happen.

Be neighborly. Reach out. Be supportive, but don't be overbearing.

Be generous. Give without being asked. Give to show that you care. Give out of love, not obligation. Give a little if you can't give a lot. Give any way you can.

Be selfless. If you can't contribute money, give of yourself. If it doesn't hurt a little, you're not giving enough.

Be realistic. Face reality and find a way to deal with the misfortune rather than withdraw from the situation.

Be forgiving. If someone is responsible for the tragedy, learn to forgive. Forgiving doesn't mean forgetting, nor does it mean approving. It just means that you're letting go of the anger.

Be reflective. Some tragedies may be preventable, so learn from mistakes. Lessons in life will be repeated until they are learned.

Be grateful. Be mindful of what really matters and appreciate what you already have.

Be hopeful. Have faith. Hope motivates you to stay the course when difficulties give you every reason to pause. Hope also has a way of saying that even a bad start can still have a happy ending.

LET A TRAGEDY BRING OUT THE BEST IN YOU

We often hear about the ills of the world, but there's little said about people who extend their hand to those they don't even know. Their kindness is overwhelming, and their generosity and cheer are both hopeful and exhilarating. Our gratitude should reflect their kindness and sacrifice.

Many of these folks are not rich and famous; they're like you and me. They're willing to lend a hand today, knowing the shoe can be on the other foot tomorrow.

How would you feel if you were in desperate need and someone you didn't even know came to your aid? You'd be overjoyed by their thoughtfulness, and their gesture would rekindle your faith in mankind. Their action would serve as a constant reminder that even though the world is large, one person *can* still make a world of difference. Be a role model that makes *you* proud. If a tragedy happens, let it bring out the best in *you*. :)

JUST BECAUSE A
PERSON IS SILENT
DOESN'T MEAN
THERE'S NO
MESSAGE.

SILENCE...
NOW HEAR THIS

It's interesting to contrast our hectic lives with the peacefulness of nature. The serenity of a stroll on a white sand beach, the calmness of a hike in a lush forest, and the stillness of wandering on a snow-covered mountain trail. The experience is tranquil, the scenery is breathtaking, and the feeling is soothing. It gives new meaning to the phrase *silence is golden*. Yet, silence is not all it's cracked up to be. In fact, silence can be a danger sign.

Silence can signal that you're contemplating — alone with your thoughts. It can indicate that you're thinking or listening — and are busy learning. But silence can also be construed as agreement or as giving approval when, in actuality, it means exactly the opposite.

THE CAUSES OF SILENCE

You'll never know if silence is harmful or innocent unless you know its origin. Here are nine causes of deafening silence:

Frightened. Some people are silent because they're afraid to speak up.

Insecure. Some folks are silent because they lack confidence and feel unworthy.

Intimidated. Some people are silent because others are monopolizing the conversation.

Emotional. Some folks are silent because they're afraid they'll regret what they say.

Enraged. Some people are silent because your words have upset them and they're sending you a message.

Disinterested. Some folks are silent out of boredom. A yawn is worth a thousand words.

Disengaged. Some people are silent because they're closing their eyes to inappropriate behavior.

Introverted. Some folks are silent because they're shy. They'd rather be a wallflower than be in the spotlight.

Apathetic. Some people are silent because they've given up — and simply don't care anymore.

BREAK THE SILENCE

If you're looking to draw people into a discussion and find out what's on their mind, here are 10 guidelines to consider:

Listen attentively. Be physically AND mentally present.

Be all ears. Give everyone a chance to speak. Don't dominate the conversation.

Take the temperature. Observe who's participating and who's not. Apathy is a silent killer.

Listen for silence. Don't assume silence means compliance. Determine if silence is a danger signal.

Draw people out. Encourage silent people to contribute to the discussion by asking for their opinion.

Make people feel special. Don't criticize or belittle viewpoints. Every idea is a good one.

Don't pull rank. It doesn't matter who comes up with an idea. Quality is what counts.

Encourage debate. Discuss differences openly, honestly, and respectfully. Focus on the message, not the messenger.

Be open-minded. Set a nonthreatening tone. Everyone is entitled to their own opinion, always recognizing that no one should force their opinion on others.

Settle differences in a cordial manner. Turning your back and walking away ends more than a conversation.

SILENCE...STOP, LOOK, AND LISTEN

Every parent knows that when little kids are too quiet in their room, it's time to check on them. That doesn't mean something's wrong, but silence can be an indication of trouble. Similarly, it doesn't matter whether you're parenting teenage kids, running a business meeting, or leading the free world, just because a person is silent doesn't mean there's no message. It could indicate absolutely nothing or it could represent the calm before the storm. You won't know unless you pay attention to what's left unsaid.

Some people drown out others to get attention. They believe that ranting is an effective communication strategy. The fact is, raised voices are rarely heard. If you're trying to exchange ideas, build trust, or engender support, you'll never know whether people are *all in* or *on the outs* unless you engage them in rich discussion. Next time you stumble upon a silent person, listen up. :)

IF IT WON'T MATTER
IN A YEAR OR TWO,
IT'S NOT WORTH
THE WORRY.

DON'T YOU WORRY
ABOUT A THING

If you're anything like me, you've worried about failing a test, being late for a meeting, or giving a lousy presentation. Well...I did crappy on some tests, arrived late for a few meetings, and you guessed it, had my share of lousy presentations. And you know what? I'm still here to tell you about it.

Sometimes we worry about events because we view them as the most important things in the world. Looking back, however, we learn that very few of these situations made a *real* difference in the long run. In sports, we win and lose games; in business, we have ups and downs; and the kids have good and bad days. Life goes on. What's more, after a few months, most situations that once seemed so important completely slip from our mind. You'd think we'd learn our lesson the next time around, but most of us treat each incident like it was our first, and we worry. After repeating this exercise again and again, some of us realize that very few things in life are really life changing.

If it won't matter in a year or two, it's not worth the worry.

WORRY ABOUT THE IMPORTANT STUFF

Here are four things to consider the next time you feel panic setting in:

Is the issue important? Keep things in perspective. Some situations appear larger than life, yet in hindsight they're inconsequential. The key is to gauge the issue beforehand. As a simple test, ask yourself whether the problem will matter in a year or two. If not, it may be unworthy of your concern.

Are you being level-headed? When you're tired, emotional, or under stress, negative thoughts can spiral out of control, even if the premise is far-fetched.

How well do you know yourself? How often do your worries actually materialize? If they *rarely* come to fruition, don't get worked up.

Can you affect the outcome? Don't worry about things that are out of your control. For example, if you're worried about the weather, let it go.

LIFE IS TOO SHORT TO WORRY

Some worrying is productive — it encourages you to be prepared, keeps you on your toes, and prevents you from letting success go to your head. In addition, it might push you to ask "What-if" questions and to create back-up plans if things go awry. Other times, worrying makes us anxious, irritable, and fearful.

Worry is a by-product of feeling powerless. We fear the unknown and are frustrated that we can't do anything about it. We also want to influence daily events even though some things are beyond our control. The key is to face that reality and go with the flow. Most things that we worry about never come to pass. And when they do, very few of them change mankind. In fact, in most cases worrying is a lot worse than the actual outcome. So, the next time you worry that the world is coming to an end, either do something about the situation or put it to rest. Take a deep breath and count to 10. If that doesn't work, count to 20. Life has its ups and downs, so make the best of the in-betweens. :)

APATHETIC PEOPLE
ARE AMONG THE
LIVING DEAD.

WHO CARES?
(I HOPE YOU DO!)

If I asked you to describe the feeling of emptiness, you might reply, "stark, gloomy, and meaningless." If I asked you to describe apathy, you might say, "a blank stare, a dwindling flame, or being emotionally absent." You might even return to the word "emptiness." Do these terms describe some people you know?

The truth is, some folks don't care about anything. They rarely get involved or pull their own weight. Plus, they have no work ethic, no sense of pride, and they invest just enough effort to squeak by. In fact, they're indifferent about most things in life. You could say that apathetic people are among the living dead.

Some folks may say, "Who cares if I'm apathetic? I'm not hurting anyone." But that's not true. They're cheating *themselves* out of the thrill of overcoming a challenge; they're depriving themselves of the satisfaction that comes with caring; and they're robbing themselves of knowing that they've made a difference.

The truth is, who cares if you speak your mind or sit in silence, win or lose, or ever try your best? *You* should! Even if you have all the talent in the world, you won't amount to anything if you don't apply yourself. As Jimmy Buffett said, "Is it ignorance or apathy? Hey, I don't know and I don't care."

DO YOU HAVE A CARE IN THE WORLD?

Look in the mirror. What's turning you off? Is apathy an isolated event or does it permeate many areas of your life? Is someone discouraging you or are *you* holding yourself back? The fact is, if you're not willing to make the commitment, don't complain about the outcome.

Leave your comfort zone. Don't wake up one day and regret that you didn't pursue your dreams because you let fear get in your way. What's worse — failing or never trying?

If you're in a rut, climb out. Stop procrastinating and get started. Dreams, unlike eggs, don't hatch from sitting on them.

Find your passion. Try something new. Start small. If it doesn't work out, limit your losses, and move on. If things go well, build on your success.

Check your attitude. Attitude is everything. Believe in your ability to make a difference. If you believe you can't...you won't.

IT'S NEVER TOO LATE TO CARE

Even though some folks show up, it's as though they're not even there. They're talented, but they don't apply themselves. They've got good ideas but never voice them. They're born leaders but choose to remain in the shadows. And even though they have dreams of grandeur, they choose to live an empty life.

The truth is, when any part of the human body hasn't exercised properly, it will atrophy. The same is true of the human spirit. If you want to get anywhere, *you* have to start somewhere. Hard work builds character, contributes to success, and promotes happiness. The world isn't going to beat a path to your door. It's easy to criticize people instead of sticking *your* neck out; it's painless to second-guess events instead of getting in the game; it's easy to blame others for your circumstances instead of accepting responsibility for your actions. The fact is, *you* have the ability to fulfill your dreams — if *you* care.

Once you know what it feels like to care, you'll never be apathetic again. As Helen Keller said, "Science may have found a cure for most evils; but it has found no remedy for the worst of them all — the apathy of human beings." People who live without caring are people who are not truly living. Who cares? I hope *you* do! You'll have no one to thank except yourself. :)

WHEN YOUR EARS
HEAR ONE THING,
BUT YOUR EYES
SEE ANOTHER...
USE YOUR BRAIN.

WHAT MAKES YOU THINK OTHERS KNOW BETTER?

We see a post on social media, read an article in the paper, listen to opinions in a meeting, hear the results of a poll, and before you know it, we adjust our views and jump on the bandwagon with everyone else. It's as if we say, "If it's good enough for them, it's good enough for me." No questions asked.

We are dramatically affected by the people around us. In fact, we tend to do things simply because others do them, rather than follow our own beliefs or think for ourselves. That's fine if we're kind, eat healthy, or read more because our friends and colleagues influence us to act that way. But this phenomenon can also compel us to do things against our own best interest — if we're not careful.

Even though being part of a group provides comfort and security, it doesn't guarantee that the group's members will always think intelligently; in fact, their reasoning may be deeply flawed. That's why you should think carefully before you end up destroying your credibility and your reputation. It's important to consider whether the messenger is credible, the information is accurate, the rationale is logical, and the intentions are honorable. The alternative is to follow the group blindly — and assume that other members did their homework.

When your ears hear one thing, but your eyes see another…use your brain.

KICK THE TIRES BEFORE YOU
BUY INTO GROUPTHINK

There are times when a group of like-minded people does irrational things because no one has the courage to step forward and scrutinize the facts, question the rationale, or examine the real motive behind the actions. Instead, everyone feeds off each other's energy until things take on a life of their own.

In retrospect, however, what if the whole idea didn't make sense? Was truth trampled? Did innocent people get hurt? Of course, you can say, you were one of many and only followed along. But does that argument hold water? The fact is, some people say and do things in a group that they'd never do themselves. You chose to be a member of the group and are responsible for your actions. So do your due diligence before taking the plunge.

Before you get swept up by groupthink, ask yourself whether joining makes sense for you. Don't let yourself get seduced by numbers, persuaded by emotion, or pressured to join. You are your own person. Don't outsource your feelings or surrender your beliefs to please others. Although it's reassuring to be part of a group, you're ultimately responsible for the choices that you make.

LISTEN TO YOUR CONSCIENCE

There are many examples of crowd mentality gone awry, such as the Salem witch trials, the Dutch tulip market bubble in the 1600s, and widespread belief at one time in a flat Earth. But there are many less glaring examples that present themselves each day. The key is to think for yourself rather than follow the herd off a cliff.

One of the biggest mistakes that people make is treating groupthink as gospel and following it blindly. It's hard to swim against the tide and stand up for your beliefs. It's tough to say "no" when others are so sure they're right. It's rough to stand alone when the quantity of the people in the group overwhelms you. But in the end, the right answer isn't always determined by the number of people who say or believe something, but rather by the *one* who has the courage and conviction to question conventional wisdom. Think before you act — others *don't* always know better. :)

IT'S NOT WHAT YOU
HAVE, BUT WHO YOU
ARE THAT COUNTS.

ARE PEOPLE INVISIBLE TO YOU?

We talk down to the waitress like she's our gofer. We shout instructions to the underling as though he's a fool. We look away from the homeless man as if he doesn't exist. To some folks, these people are invisible.

Did you ever consider that these people have pride like you and me, they have feelings like you and me, and they have desires like you and me? In fact, we're alike on so many levels because when you look beneath the surface, we all want many of the same things in life. Yet some don't see it that way. If they don't look like us, they must be dangerous; if they don't sound like us, they must be ignorant; and if they don't agree with us, they must be evil.

Don't judge people you don't know.

DIVISION DOESN'T ADD UP

Do power, money, and status make someone better? Do they give anyone the right to be arrogant, disrespectful, or rude? I think not. While accomplishments indicate that people are successful, they don't give anyone the right to dehumanize others and treat them as second-class citizens.

One of the reasons this occurs is due to divisions that we intentionally create or that are thrust upon us. Instead of emphasizing commonalities that bring people together, we *artificially* separate ourselves into distinct groups that accentuate our differences.

> Branded luxury goods are high-quality products and services that appeal to a person's ego and self-worth. They shout, "I'm successful so I can afford these." If people buy luxury goods to reward themselves for a job well done, that's fine. But when a "toy" is flaunted, it creates a divide between the haves and the have-nots. While some people show off material excess, others are having trouble putting food on the table.

> First-class seating, corner offices, and reserved parking are all ways of saying "I'm important." But these perks also can create walls between people.

> Some people profit from dividing us. They pit us against one another by asserting that some folks hold an unfair advantage. According to them, the real determinant of success is one's "label," rather than one's character, ability, or performance. If you're not a member of the "chosen few," you don't stand a fighting chance to be successful. This drives a wedge between us. It makes people feel bitter, envious, and disillusioned.

THE CURE FOR WHAT DIVIDES US

If your success was earned through hard work and honesty, don't apologize for it. There's nothing wrong with living the good life. You've earned it. But if you think power, money, and status give you the right to be rude, disrespectful, or condescending, you've got it all wrong. No one should be treated like they're invisible.

The truth is, while power, money, and status indicate that you're successful, it's not *what you have* but *who you are* that counts. Treating people with dignity and respect says more about you than trying to prove how important you are. Living with honor says more about you than achieving your wealth by selling your soul. Making a difference in people's lives says more about you than enriching your own life. As John Wooden, the legendary college basketball coach, said, "Be more concerned with your character than your reputation, because your character is what you really are, while your reputation is merely what others think you are." Be the person who sees the best in people, makes them feel good about themselves, and brightens their day. Bring the invisible people out into the light. You'll be a positive force for good in their lives, *and* you'll feel good about yourself, too. :)

SOMETIMES YOU
DESERVE A PAT ON
THE BACK, EVEN IF
YOU HAVE TO DO IT
YOURSELF.

GIVE YOURSELF A PAT ON THE BACK

Some people are perfectionists; they consider anything short of perfection a failure. Instead of celebrating the important progress they're making to achieve their goals, they focus on their shortcomings, as well as on all the work that still remains to be completed.

The problem is that constantly looking for and belittling yourself for minor infractions is debilitating and can negatively impact your confidence over time. That's why it's important to recognize and reward your progress as you strive for excellence. One of the best ways to build your self-esteem is to identify wins and give yourself a pat on the back each day. That will help you build confidence as you strive to achieve your long-term goals.

25 REASONS WHY YOU'RE AWESOME

Sometimes you deserve a pat on the back, even if you have to do it yourself. Identify 10 reasons to pat yourself on the back — each day — using the list below.

Did you:

> Step outside your comfort zone?

> Refuse to let a problem ruin your day?

Help a stranger in need?

Maintain willpower rather than surrender to temptation?

Knock *key* items off your to-do list?

Ask for help rather than go it alone?

Make someone feel good about him- or herself?

Complete a task that you despise?

Listen to your conscience?

Put someone's interests ahead of your own?

Perform a favor without asking for something in return?

Run toward a problem rather than away from it?

Barrel through a tough assignment?

Cast aside your fears and go for it?

Forgive someone who disappointed you?

Keep your calm while others lost their heads?

See the positive when others saw only the negative?

Delegate tasks rather than maintain tight control?

Remain determined rather than quit?

Juggle several balls without getting flustered?

Comfort a friend during a rough patch?

Exceed your own expectations?

Advocate for yourself rather than keep silent?

Overcome an obstacle?

Accept responsibility rather than cast blame?

A DOSE OF REALITY

Some people see a glass as half-full; others see it as half-empty. Your view of the world will have a significant impact on your behavior — as well as on your mental attitude, confidence, and your self-worth. It will ultimately determine your success and happiness.

When you praise yourself for being awesome, you're not telling a fib; you're doing wonderful things every day. The problem is that *you choose* not to see it, much less compliment yourself for a job well done. How would you feel if you did something awesome for someone and they chose not to recognize it? Don't you deserve the same respect from yourself?

Be nice to yourself. If you're oblivious to the wonderful things that you do each day, force yourself to see them. Conversely, if you're not doing enough wonderful things, this may encourage you to do more. One of the nicest gifts that you can give someone is a sincere compliment. Maybe it's time to start talking to yourself. You're awesome! Give yourself a pat on the back. :)

PREPARE IN
THE MORNING;
REFLECT AT NIGHT.

MAKE EXPERIENCE YOUR BEST TEACHER

After a sporting event, did you ever ask someone how they did? Their common response is either "We won," or "We lost." While their answer is factually correct, it doesn't tell the *complete* story. For example, they could have led the whole game or made an exciting comeback, performed their best or lost due to mistakes, won by a landslide or lost by a hair. The point is, while winning or losing, being right or wrong, doing well or poorly, describes the outcome, results rarely tell the *entire* story. The world is rarely black or white; we learn by examining the gray areas. You have to dig beneath the surface to learn from your experience.

PREPARE IN THE MORNING; REFLECT AT NIGHT

Learning through experience will help you grow personally and professionally; it'll prevent mistakes from returning for an encore; and it'll help you determine if you're on course in achieving your goals. Learning from experience doesn't happen in a vacuum. You have to take the initiative, be open to your findings, and be willing to modify your behavior to yield results.

Life is a classroom. There are many opportunities to reflect on your growth. For example, you can assess your actions at the end of the day, at the completion of a project, or after a failure. You can assess your progress at the end of the year or after reaching an important milestone. The key is to pause…and learn, before marching on.

LIVE AND LEARN

Here are 20 questions that you may want to consider:

Reflect on an activity

Did you do your best?

Were you adequately prepared?

What surprised you most?

Did you ask more of others than you were willing to do yourself?

Did you value other people's opinions more than your own?

Were you thinking rationally or did your emotions get the best of you?

Did you spend more time talking or listening?

Did you build trust or squander it?

Did you accept responsibility for the choices that you made?

What would you do differently next time?

Reflect on your goals

Are your priorities receiving adequate attention?

Are you more talk or more action?

Are you being guided by your values?

Do you value possessions more than relationships?

Do you spend more time doing what you *have to* versus what you *want to*?

Do you give more than you take?

Are you taking anything or anyone for granted?

Would you be happy if your kids mimicked your behavior?

Do you follow your own advice?

What's holding you back?

CHALK IT UP TO EXPERIENCE

This isn't a call to drive yourself crazy or to dissect every move that you make, but rather to consciously pause, from time to time, and reflect on your behavior. Additionally, this isn't a call to beat yourself up, but to give yourself constructive feedback that will help you learn and grow.

Some folks may be thinking, "I don't have the time. I have a busy life." The truth is, you don't have to set aside a lot of time to do this. Learning through experience is a mindset more than an activity. We develop routine behaviors to help ourselves manage daily life. As time goes by, behaviors become habits that are imprinted in our subconscious. Wouldn't you like to know if your habits are helping or hurting your growth? Or would you rather repeat mistakes and charge full speed ahead? Ask yourself, do you have 20 years of experience or one year of experience repeated 20 times? Stop and think. Make experience your best teacher. :)

IF SOMEONE
CHOOSES TO LIVE
A CERTAIN WAY, AND
IT DOESN'T INFRINGE
ON ANYONE'S
FREEDOM, IT'S THEIR
CHOICE TO MAKE.

SHOULD YOUR OPINION MATTER MORE THAN MINE?

It's great that you live a healthy lifestyle, are passionate about your beliefs, and are committed to your causes, but that doesn't mean everyone has to agree with you. Believe me, no one's trying to pass judgment; quite to the contrary. Unlike multiple-choice tests, in life there may be two right answers to the same question.

Folks know what's right for them. They have strong beliefs and are passionate about their values, too. Most people don't mind when others ask them to follow their lead every once in a while, but forcing one's opinion on folks makes everyone feel uncomfortable.

> If someone chooses to live a certain way, and it doesn't infringe on anyone's freedom, it's their choice to make.

MY WAY OR THE HIGHWAY

A true friend is one who respects a friend for who he or she is…not just if that friend shares the same viewpoints. Sometimes, however, it's not that simple — especially when one's beliefs and values encroach on another's freedom. Rather than striving to seek compromise, it seems that the new standard of discourse is "My way or the highway." This shortsighted and ultimately destructive attitude is a "lose-lose" for everyone.

The fact is, we live in a world that's getting smaller every day. We can't expect others to abandon their values any more than we would forsake our own. It's important to be tolerant of other people's cultures and values, recognizing that no one has the right to force his or her way of life on anyone else.

BUILDING BRIDGES . . .

This does not mean that people should abandon their beliefs. This process, however, must be civil and respectful of others' views.

Here are 10 considerations to promote an amicable discussion:

When a disagreement arises, all discussion should focus on the merits of each position, without denigration of others. There's no need to either disparage anyone or resort to personal attacks.

Timely and accurate information is an important ingredient of successful debate. As Daniel Patrick Moynihan once said, "Everyone is entitled to his own opinion, but not to his own facts."

Many "battles" don't have winners and losers — there are just losers. Don't look for ways to back an opponent into a corner. Instead, find ways to let each side save face.

Take the high ground. Remain open-minded. Look for common ground. Identify ways to compromise and find win-win opportunities.

Put yourself in the other person's shoes. Try to find the merit in each other's arguments.

Communication is a two-way street. It requires more than talking. Remember, there's a difference between listening and hearing.

Although it may take longer, it's better to achieve buy-in than to be overpowering in order to achieve a short-term gain.

Present both sides of an argument to ensure that you're objective and fair.

Relationships prosper when everyone benefits. Prepare to concede short-term wins to secure long-term gains. Ensure that actions lead to mutual gains.

Never dance in the end zone when you score points. It'll only damage the process going forward.

BE PREPARED TO HEAL THYSELF

It's important to build relationships on what unites us rather than what divides us. We should abandon any practice that pits us against one another.

I long for a day when leaders bring us together rather than divide us; when people strive to better themselves rather than trying to change others; when fairness and tolerance replace weapons disguised as words; when we measure success not by what people accumulate in life, but by what they're able to give back. And when win-win relationships define success, rather than winning at all costs.

Before we can make this a reality, keep in mind the wisdom of Bill Bluestein, the corporate executive, who said, "Before you try to change others, remember how hard it is to change yourself." But this is all my opinion. :)

YOU HAVE TO LIVE
WITH YOURSELF
FOR THE REST
OF YOUR LIFE.

HOW TO MAKE THE
TOUGHEST DECISIONS
IN THE WORLD

Think of the toughest decision you ever made. It was probably highly visible, of critical importance, and of course, the result wasn't going to be popular. To make matters worse, you probably felt as though your neck was on the line and there would be consequences if things went south. It's also tough when you're forced to make a decision that could cause people pain — even if the outcome would be in everyone's best interest. In each of these circumstances, those with strong moral character took a deep breath and met the challenge boldly. They chose to do the right thing.

But other people don't see it that way. *Their* primary focus is how the decision will impact them personally. What's more, they formulate a plan to CYA if the result doesn't turn out as planned. They're likely to limit their risk by following majority opinion, opting for a joint decision, or kicking the can down the road. They could care less whether or not it's the right thing to do — it's right for them. Period!

Ask yourself, "Do I care not only about where life has taken me, but also about how I got there?" I've learned that you'll rarely regret a decision if it was logical and fair, and you knew in your heart that it was morally defensible. The truth is, *knowing* what's right isn't as important as *doing* what's right.

DO GOOD PEOPLE FINISH FIRST?

Some people may say, "While all of this sounds great in theory, you're living in a fantasy world." They believe you have to be tough and put yourself first. To that I say "hogwash." You be the judge:

Relationships. When you're a person of high moral character, others won't have to second-guess your decisions or question your motives. It's abundantly clear that your heart is in the right place and that your intent is honorable. This strengthens the bonds of trust and creates healthy and productive relationships.

Leadership. When you base decisions on doing the right thing rather than on what's politically expedient, you'll earn the trust, respect, and admiration of your colleagues. People will follow you because you have moral authority rather than because you wield power and position.

Business success. When you strive for win-win decisions rather than winner-take-all, the trust and commitment that you build will translate into significant competitive advantage for business. The truth is, there is a direct correlation between integrity and the bottom line.

Reputation. When you live your life with honor, you'll secure the trust and respect of others. Your reputation is like a shadow, following you wherever you go. You can't disguise it, you can't hide from it, and you certainly can't run from it. It will follow you for life. And although it's said that you can't be in two places at the same time, you actually do it every day — your reputation serves as your stand-in whenever you're not around. Your reputation can be your best friend or your worst enemy. What does your decision-making process say about you?

Face the facts. When you live by sound principles and choose to do the right thing, you'll face yourself in the mirror each day and be proud of what you see. You'll be able to say that no matter the consequences, you did the right thing. "How much is that worth," you ask? You have to live with yourself for the rest of your life. Follow your conscience. Sleep well. :)

"

PEOPLE WHO LOOK
UP TO YOU WATCH
EVERY MOVE THAT
YOU MAKE —
SO DON'T LET
THEM DOWN.

DO YOU LEAD
BY EXAMPLE?

You are being watched every minute of every day. Sounds creepy, right? But it's true. Every word that you say and every move that you make is being carefully followed. What's more…you can't escape it. Here are the facts.

It doesn't matter whether you're young or old, rich or poor, launching your career or known as the "big cheese" — your words and actions have a huge impact on your credibility and reputation. Plus, they're influencing others in ways you've never imagined. Are you proud of the message that you send to others? If not, it might be time to reexamine your behavior.

> People who look up to you watch every move that you make —
> so don't let them down.

30 WAYS TO LEAD BY EXAMPLE

Sometimes it's clear as day that you're sending people a message; other times, it may not be that obvious. Here are 30 ways to walk the talk:

Be the first to give rather than the first to take.

Earn trust and respect rather than demanding it.

Get in the game rather than watching from the sidelines.

Think for yourself rather than acting like a parrot.

Do your best rather than doing just enough to get by.

Man up rather than ducking your responsibility.

Think "we" rather than "me."

Lead the way rather than just talking a good game.

Build people up rather than tearing them down.

Confront poor behavior rather than turning a blind eye.

Remain true to your values rather than blowing with the wind.

Pull your own weight rather than asking others to do double duty.

Run toward problems rather than away from them.

Admit mistakes rather than casting blame.

Offer solutions rather than just complaining.

Follow your moral compass rather than asking to be shown the way.

Go to the back of the line rather than cutting in front.

Tell it like it is rather than beating around the bush.

Build bridges rather than constructing walls.

Raise your own hand rather than volunteering others.

Keep an open mind rather than shutting the door.

Do what you can rather than making excuses why you can't.

Leave your comfort zone rather than surrendering to your fears.

Raise the bar rather than accepting mediocrity.

Be strong-minded rather than quitting at the first sign of trouble.

Better yourself rather than trying to change others.

Honor your word rather than breaking your promise.

Stand strong rather than bending to peer pressure.

Listen to your conscience rather than selling your soul.

Make a difference in others' lives rather than enriching your own.

WANTED: ROLE MODELS

Your behavior defines who you are and what you stand for. It reveals your upbringing, reflects on the organization that you represent, and it paints a lasting impression — your reputation — that is as hard to shake as your shadow.

Do you follow your conscience? Is your handshake as binding as a contract? Can friends count on you in good times and bad? Do you treat people who *can't* do something for you as well as you treat those who *can*? Would you be proud if your kids followed in your footsteps? If you can't say yes to these questions, ask yourself *why*.

If you want to raise kids with strong moral character, strengthen your organization's culture, or encourage citizens to be productive members of society, don't look to change *their* behavior, examine your own. Ask yourself whether your actions are having a positive or negative impact on the people around you. Are you guiding them toward a righteous path or steering them down a dead end? You're a role model. Act like one. :)

WHEN YOU'RE NOT
AROUND, YOUR
REPUTATION WILL
SPEAK FOR YOU.

WHAT DOES YOUR NAME SAY ABOUT YOU?

When you were born, your parents chose a name for you. They knew it was an important decision because it would identify you for life. Your name, however, is only a label; it isn't half as important as what it represents. The fact is, although many people may share the same name, your reputation is yours and yours alone.

Your reputation doesn't happen by chance. It's a reflection of who you are and how you choose to live your life. What do you want your name to say about you? Do you want it to say that you're a giver or a taker? You're a hard worker or a slacker? You're a loyal companion or a fair-weather friend? You're as honest as the day is long or you have trouble with the truth?

When you're not around, your reputation will speak for you.

YOUR NAME IS YOUR CALLING CARD

In years past, when we lived in small communities, your reputation was confined to a tight circle. Today however, with the advent of social media, your words and actions can go viral with the touch of a button. That has serious consequences — your reputation can be your best friend or your worst enemy. It can open doors to marvelous opportunities or ensure that every door is slammed right in your face.

Your reputation tells the world who you *really* are. It will tell others whether they can place their trust in you, whether you're easy to do business with, and whether you keep your commitments. It will also tell them if you're selfish, if they have to keep an eye on you, and if you're a bad influence. Ouch! The good news is that your reputation isn't the result of luck; it's a direct consequence of what you say and do. Protect your reputation like it's the most valuable asset you own. Because it is!

MAKE A NAME FOR YOURSELF

"How do I build a good name for myself?" you ask. Some folks may advise you to manage your personal brand. The truth is, building a reputation isn't about *managing* your brand; it's about doing what's right to begin with. Your reputation is based on the cumulative sum of your words and actions. The more consistent your behavior is, the greater clarity you're providing to others. That will leave no doubt in anyone's mind who you are and what you represent.

Some folks think they can fool others by saying one thing and doing another. While you may be able to mislead someone in the short term, it'll ultimately come back to bite you. And when it does, you'll be forced to do damage control. If you think that's worth the risk, you're sadly mistaken. The fact is that it's much harder to repair a damaged reputation than to build a good one in the first place — you can't unring a bell.

Even though trust takes a long time to build, restoring it takes even longer. First, you have to be forgiven; next, you have to break down emotional walls; and last, you have to prove that you're worthy of trust and respect. That doesn't happen overnight — people aren't quick to forget.

Even though your reputation may be as good as gold, what matters most is that you feel good about yourself and *you're* proud of what your name stands for. Do you care not only about where life has taken you, but about how you got there? That means setting high standards, living with honor and integrity, and holding yourself accountable for your behavior. It means shifting your mindset from "I may be able to get away with it," to letting your conscience be your guide. It doesn't matter how other people view you if you can't face the mirror each day. It's your life to live. Own it! You have to live with yourself for the rest of your life. :)

YOU DON'T HAVE
TO BE RICH TO GIVE;
YOUR GIFT CAN BE
AS SIMPLE
AS A SMILE.

BEING GENEROUS
DOESN'T COST A PENNY

It's better to give than to receive. But some folks never got that message. Instead, they claim they're in no position to give. You've got to wonder if they're being truthful or if it's just a convenient excuse. In any case, generosity doesn't require giving lavish gifts or money; it can simply mean giving of oneself. You don't have to be rich to give; your gift can be as simple as a smile.

Therefore, it isn't a question of whether you're *able* to give, it's whether you *will* give.

THE JOY OF GIVING

Generous people know that you gain so much satisfaction from giving. The only limiting factor is your imagination. There are many ways to give. For example, you can give someone: advice, encouragement, appreciation, trust, hope, an opportunity, your opinion, your undivided attention, a shoulder to cry on, and of course, respect. The point is that the opportunity to give is endless.

It's not *what* you give, but rather *that* you give.

10 WAYS TO SHOW THAT YOU CARE

It doesn't require an arm and a leg to be generous. Here are 10 guidelines to get you started:

Give from your heart. Give out of kindness, not obligation.

Give for no particular reason. Don't wait for a special occasion. Every day is an opportunity to be generous.

Give without being asked. Step up to the plate *before* someone makes a request of you. Surprise them with your kindness.

Give any way you can. Give a little if you can't give a lot. But remember, if giving that gift doesn't hurt a little — you're not giving enough.

Give without strings attached. Give without expecting something in return. Your reward should *not* result in personal gain but in making others happy.

Give of yourself. Lavish gifts are not a substitute for caring. Give of your time, talent, or expertise.

Give to show that you care. Be available in times of need. Lend an ear or a shoulder to cry on.

Give without creating dependency. Instill self-reliance. Teach someone "how to fish" rather than making them dependent on your benevolence.

Give to those who need it most. There are people less fortunate than you. Make a difference in their life.

Give without attracting attention. Be humble. Don't make a spectacle out of your generosity.

GENEROSITY: THE MORE YOU GIVE, THE MORE YOU RECEIVE

If you're asking yourself what stops people from giving, the answer is simple. Some people are self-centered. They're more interested in feeding their own ego than in nourishing someone else. Some folks claim they're busy — busy focusing on their own needs. Others are simply selfish. They'd rather get something they *don't* need than give to someone in need. What they fail to realize is that when you exude good energy, it often comes right back to you — full circle — like a boomerang. But the real reward is feeling good about yourself and knowing that you're making a difference.

Be generous in your own special way. You don't have to do something life changing to make a difference. Your gift need not come in a box. Your deed can be as simple as making someone feel special, reaching out to a lonely person, helping a troubled kid find the right path, or comforting a friend. It can take the form of giving someone confidence, slowing down to provide quality time to someone, or sharing an honest opinion. The result is that you'll change the world one good deed at a time. What do you have to lose? Being generous doesn't cost a penny. :)

KARMA IS LIKE
A BOOMERANG.
I HOPE YOU HAVE
MANY HAPPY
RETURNS.

KARMA: MAKE YOUR OWN LUCK

Sometimes I see people do things and I shake my head, thinking, "What's wrong with them? What are they thinking?" Some of those folks believe that rules don't apply to them or that they're above the law. Others think their deeds won't catch up with them. The truth is, they may get away with "murder" for a week, a month, or even years. BUT, as long as karma exists, people ultimately get what they deserve.

Karma isn't always bad. In fact, it's the natural law of cause and effect. Simply put, karma means "what goes around comes around." If you emit good energy, it'll come back full circle — like a boomerang. The same holds true for negative behavior.

If you want good karma,* you not only have to *do good*, but you must *be good*. In fact, good karma is created through your *thoughts* and *intentions*, as well as your *deeds*. In other words, good begets good.

Karma is like a boomerang. I hope you have many happy returns.

KARMA: GOOD THINGS HAPPEN FOR A REASON (BAD THINGS, TOO)

Here are eight powerful reasons to invest in *your* karma:

Create better self-esteem. Take great pride knowing that you're a person of high moral character.

Produce stronger relationships. Maintain fair, honest, trusting, and selfless relationships because people mirror the treatment they receive from you.

Build a solid reputation. Gain the trust of others because people know what you stand for and that you continuously exhibit honorable behavior.

Generate lower stress levels. Reduce anxiety because you don't carry the guilt and shame of leading a disreputable life.

Retain a clear conscience. Get a good night's sleep knowing that your intentions are always admirable and your behavior is just.

Attain greater happiness. Gain satisfaction knowing that you give more than you take, that you bring out the best in others, that you make a difference in people's lives, and that you help make the world a better place.

Achieve greater success. Get what you deserve. Luck is nothing more than good karma doing its job.

Enjoy a greater sense of purpose. Achieve true happiness knowing that you live a virtuous life.

DON'T LOOK NOW, BUT
YOUR KARMA IS WATCHING

When some people do things, they often have an "angle." They *want* or *expect* something in return. If you think you can trick karma by concealing your motives or performing a few niceties, you've got it all wrong. It's not enough to go through the motions of doing a good deed every once in a blue moon; it's your motive that counts.

It comes down to the way you choose to view and live your life. We're all part of a world in which everything is connected and interrelated. If your thoughts, intentions, and deeds are heartfelt and beneficial to others, you will produce good karma. When you do something thoughtful, however, do it for the right reason. Make sure your intention is honorable and your motive is pure. That will furnish all the benefits good karma offers. The next time you think you can't make your own luck, remember your karma, and think again! :)

*It's important to note that I'm using the term *karma* in a spiritual rather than a religious sense.

YOU MAY NOT BE
ABLE TO CHANGE
THE WORLD,
BUT YOU CAN
CHANGE THE WORLD
AROUND YOU.

CHANGE A LIFE AND YOU MAY END UP CHANGING YOURS

Think about a person who's had a tremendous impact on your life. It may be your Mom or Dad who believed in you, the coach who inspired you, the teacher who guided you in the right direction, the boss who gave you your first big opportunity, or the friend who's always been by your side. I'm sure when you think of that person, it brings a huge smile to your face — as it should.

You may say that some of these folks were just doing their job. True. But even though you've had several good teachers, coaches, and bosses over the years, I'm sure a few of them really stand out from the crowd. You remember their passion, dedication, kindness, and, of course, their generosity. After all, they changed your life!

That obviously begs the question…are *you* leaving a lasting impact on others? It only takes one person to change a life — and that one person may as well be you.

MAKE A DIFFERENCE

Whether you're aware of it or not, you're touching the lives of people every day. What can you do to step up your game?

Be an exemplary role model. Lead by example. Demonstrate that character is the DNA of success and happiness.

Be an awesome parent. Having kids is not the same as being a parent. Raise your kids to be kind, productive, and self-reliant; to make good choices and to be personally responsible for their actions; to pursue their purpose with gusto; and to live their life with honor and dignity.

Be a humble leader. Share your success. As you climb the ladder of success, reach down and pull others up with you.

Be a dedicated mentor. Take someone under your wing and show them the ropes. Give the kind of advice that they won't hear anywhere else.

Be a compassionate boss. Show your employees that work isn't all business. Build trusting relationships. Make yourself available and supportive in times of need.

Be a shrewd businessperson. Develop win-win rather than winner-take-all relationships. Prove that there's more to go around when you grow a large pie, together, than when you squabble to divide a smaller one.

Be a *real* friend. Demonstrate loyalty when someone's chips are down and no one else has their back.

Be an inspiration. Set high expectations and push people beyond their capabilities. Show confidence in them when they're having a weak moment.

Be perceptive. Give someone the big break they need in life. See someone's potential even when others are blind to their promise.

Be tough, but fair. Make people accountable for their actions. They'll thank you one day.

Be available. Give the gift of time. Lend a shoulder to cry on when someone needs a friendly ear or support during tough times.

Be the better person. Be the first to give, the first to forgive, the first to compromise, and the first to say "I'm sorry."

Be even-handed. Stand up for injustice, speak up for the less fortunate, and don't give up on fairness and tolerance.

Be a loving spouse. Put your heart into your marriage. Share your hopes and your fears, your laughter and your tears, your joy and your sorrow.

CHANGE A LIFE FOREVER

Think of your greatest accomplishments. Where would changing someone's life rank on your list? Consider: If they hadn't crossed paths with you, they wouldn't be the person they are, they wouldn't have the opportunities they have, and they wouldn't be positioned to achieve their hopes and dreams. Bravo! You made a difference! As an added bonus, change someone's life and you may end up changing yours.

Why complain about the ills of the world when you could be a world of difference to someone you know? You may not be able to change the world, but you can change the world around you. Change a life and create a ripple that cascades forever. :)

ONE PERSON CAN
MAKE ALL THE
DIFFERENCE. AND
THAT ONE PERSON
IS YOU!

THE POWER OF ONE

Sometimes we feel the world is so large and complex that it's impossible for any one of us to make a difference. When something comes up that requires action, we think, "I'm only one person. What can I do anyway?" The result is that we sit back and wait for others to make the first move — that is, if anyone else is willing to make the effort.

BUT, what if we tried? What if we shed our fears and inhibitions and others did so as well? What if we challenged ourselves to stand up and be counted, and we each made a difference in our own special way? Or, better yet, what if enough people stepped forward and accepted the challenge along with us? The truth is, we might be able to change the world. As Steve Jobs said, "The people who are crazy enough to think they can change the world are the ones who do."

YOU CAN MAKE A DIFFERENCE (IF YOU TRY)

Still unconvinced that one person can make a difference? Tell that to the angel who saved the patient's life by donating her organ, to the craftsman who helped his poor neighbor by rebuilding their weather-torn home, or to the couple who showed the true meaning of love by adopting a foster child. They gave of themselves and are changing lives as a result.

You don't have to do something life-changing to make a difference. Your deed can be as simple as making someone feel special, reaching out to a lonely person, helping a troubled kid find the right path, or comforting a friend who needs a shoulder to cry on. The fact is that you'll be changing the world one good deed at a time.

DREAMS, UNLIKE EGGS, DON'T HATCH FROM SITTING ON THEM

Let all the toxic people complain up a storm, let the naysayers say that it can't be done. The truth is, you can't (or should I say, won't) make a difference if you don't try. Here are four guidelines to keep in mind:

Believe. Have faith that one person can make a difference, and that one person is you.

Act. There are opportunities all around you. Don't wait for someone else to make the first move. Choose one and do something about it.

Lead. Be the change that you want to see in the world. Don't just talk a good game. Lead the way.

Transform. Throw a pebble into the water and create ripples. Little wins create momentum; consistency can turn into lasting change.

DON'T LOOK TO OTHERS; LOOK TO YOURSELF

Think what would happen if everyone shouted out their window at the same time. The sound would be unnerving. Now think of the impact that we could have if we collectively made someone feel special, mentored a colleague, or helped a person in need. The impact would be astounding.

There is power in numbers. One person can get things started; a second person can create some momentum; a third person may influence others to join in. And, before you know it, you've created a movement.

The world is changing every day. If enough people create a ripple for change, we can create a better future. Your choice: Complain about all the things that are wrong or be the person who helps to make them right. One person can make all the difference. And that one person is YOU! :)

RESOURCES

DO YOU GRUMBLE
ABOUT THINGS OR
WORK TO MAKE
THEM BETTER?

WILL YOU CHOOSE THE RIGHT PATH?

Next time you forget that you're the captain of your ship, think about the choices that you make every day and the impact that they have on your life. While some of your decisions have short-term consequences, others will shadow you for life.

Do you:

1. Surround yourself with positive role models or negative influencers?

2. Listen to your conscience or fall victim to temptation?

3. Satisfy your needs or try to please everyone else?

4. Leave your comfort zone or become paralyzed by fear?

5. Put first things first or treat everything as a priority?

6. Set high expectations or settle for mediocrity?

7. Learn every day or allow yourself to become stale?

8. Crave instant gratification or invest in your future?

9. Forgive and forget or harbor anger?

10. Jump right in or put things off?

11. Keep your promises or break your commitments?

12. Do your best or just check off items as complete?

13. Accept personal responsibility or make excuses?

14. Appreciate what you have or continually reach for more?

15. Stand up for your beliefs or blow with the wind?

16. Delegate responsibility or maintain tight control?

17. Accept adversity like a champ or feel sorry for yourself?

18. Grumble about things or work to make them better?

19. Live in the present or relive the past?

20. Simplify your life or settle for complexity?

21. Go it alone or seek assistance from others?

22. Follow the rules or act like a maverick?

23. Admit that things are beyond your control or beat your head against the wall?

24. Think win-win or conspire to get the upper hand?

25. Speak out against injustice or expect others to do the heavy lifting?

26. Voice your opinion or maintain silence?

27. Seek the truth or allow yourself to be swayed by public opinion?

28. Give it all you've got or surrender to a moment of weakness?

29. Maintain an open mind or cling to long-standing viewpoints?

30. Protect what you have or risk it all?

31. Recognize when to say "no" or serve as a doormat?

32. Volunteer yourself or wait for others to raise their hand?

33. Second-guess your decisions or move forward with confidence?

34. Hold your head high or criticize and belittle yourself?

35. Believe you control your destiny or think you're a victim of circumstance?

The future you get depends on the choices you make. Choose the right path. :)

DO YOU INVEST
YOUR TIME
OR SPEND IT?

WHERE DID THE TIME GO?

1. Those who waste the most time are usually the first to complain of having too little.

2. Being busy is not the same as being productive.

3. Do you repeat mistakes or learn from them?

4. Do you invest your time or spend it?

5. If everything is a priority, nothing is a priority.

6. Urgent is not the same as important.

7. Do little daily distractions sidetrack you from getting big things done?

8. Do you spend more time stressing about what has to be done or doing it?

9. Do you start everything from scratch?

10. Do you get easily overwhelmed and become unproductive?

11. Do you gravitate to things that you enjoy or to your priorities?

12. How many times do you redo something because you rushed it the first time?

13. Do you let other people hijack your time?

14. Do you believe in preventative maintenance or wait until things break down?

15. Do you address small problems before they get BIG?

16. Do you anticipate situations or react to them?

17. Do you spend more time lighting fires or putting them out?

18. Do you buy time by getting less sleep and then lose time because you're overtired?

19. Do you buy things only to return them later?

20. After making decisions, do you look forward or backward?

21. How much valuable time do you waste trying to save a few dollars?

22. Are you productive while you're waiting for people?

23. Do you settle for excellence or strive for perfection?

24. Are you conscious of how you spend your time?

25. Do you help everyone except yourself?

26. Do you call three times or leave a voicemail?

27. Do you buy cheap merchandise and replace it regularly?

28. How many times do you read something before acting on it?

29. The two greatest time-savers are saying "I don't know" and "I was wrong."

30. Do you fill up your gas tank or make several stops each week?

31. Do you complete the next item on the to-do list or what's most important?

32. Do you cancel meetings if there's nothing to discuss, or do you meet because it's on your calendar?

33. Do you ask all your questions at once or go back again and again?

34. Do you stress over things that can't be changed?

35. Do you spend more time building relationships or mending them?

36. How much time do you spend looking for things?

37. Do you consolidate similar activities to save time?

38. Do you learn anything after running into a wall? (Or do you run into it again?)

39. Do you take time to smell the roses? If not, both you and your nose will be missing out.

40. Do you insist on approving everything, yet are unavailable to review anything?

41. Does your schedule conflict with your priorities?

42. Do you set aside quality time for your family?

43. Do you measure achievement by the time that you put into something or by the value that you provide?

44. Do you say "no" to some ideas so that you can say "yes" to others?

45. Do you take the time to reflect on your day?

46. Do you schedule downtime when you can pause…and reflect?

47. Do you focus on doing things right or on doing the right things?

48. Do you have more on your to-do list than you can possibly do?

49. Do you strategize the most efficient way to get things done?

50. Do you select one thing to accomplish each day? :)

CHECKING ITEMS
OFF A TO-DO LIST
DOESN'T DETERMINE
PROGRESS;
FOCUSING ON
YOUR PRIORITIES
IS WHAT COUNTS.

HOW TO TACKLE
YOUR TO-DO LIST

It's so easy for a to-do list to snowball out of control. In some cases, it takes no time at all to go from "I can do this," to outright panic. In fact, it can become so overwhelming that it makes you freeze in your tracks — preventing you from getting *anything* done. Here are eight strategies to help you get it done:

Start with priorities. Remember, everything on your to-do list is *not* a priority. Checking items off a to-do list doesn't determine progress; focusing on your priorities is what counts.

Don't give it a second thought. Sometimes the hardest thing to do is to get started. So fight the urge to overthink everything. Jump right in without delay.

Limit distractions. Don't let anything or anyone sidetrack you. Focus on your task at hand. Whatever is "calling" you will be there when you're finished.

Learn from mistakes. Be aware of how you procrastinate and learn from it. When people don't learn from mistakes, their actions often turn into bad habits.

Set a short-term goal. Make a commitment to yourself — even an artificial deadline. A goal forces us to get things done.

Break big activities down into small pieces. Don't get overwhelmed by the magnitude of a task. Big problems are best solved in small pieces.

Fire the perfectionist. You'll rarely have all the information you need to make a "perfect" decision. So don't demand perfection. The philosopher Voltaire warned against letting the perfect be the enemy of the good. That advice still holds true today.

Think about it. Be conscious of your thoughts. Try to replace counter-productive thoughts with positive ones that motivate you and keep you on task. :)

SOMETIMES THE
HARDEST THING
TO DO IS TO
GET STARTED.

IT'S NOT ENOUGH TO
DELEGATE A TASK.
GIVE THE PERSON
THE RESPONSIBILITY
AND AUTHORITY
TO GET IT DONE.

10 PROVEN WAYS TO DELEGATE

Leave your comfort zone. If you don't feel comfortable delegating, you're not alone. Change is difficult. Think about it this way…if we didn't try to walk, we'd all still be crawling.

Know what matters most. Set priorities and determine which trade-offs are right for you.

Build trust. Surround yourself with talented people who possess a high level of trust and integrity.

Manage the process. Focus on the process as much as on the end result. And make sure to consider strengths and weaknesses when assigning work.

Be explicit about goals and expectations. Tell people your ultimate goal rather than micromanaging how they do it. Who knows…they may come up with a better way.

Set milestones. Delegating does *not* mean walking away from an activity until it's complete. Establish key milestones and review progress along the way.

Delegate responsibility *and* authority. It's not enough to delegate a task. Give the person the responsibility and authority to get it done.

Set the right tone. Create an environment in which dialog is open, questions are encouraged, and mistakes become part of a learning experience.

Give continual feedback. Remember, there's a difference between criticism and constructive feedback.

Recognize and reward excellence. Give credit where credit is due. Compliment people in public; criticize them in private. :)

TELL PEOPLE YOUR
ULTIMATE GOAL
RATHER THAN
MICROMANAGING
HOW THEY DO IT.

THOSE WHO BEGIN
THINGS, BUT NEVER
COMPLETE THEM,
ACCOMPLISH
NOTHING.

12 REASONS WHY PEOPLE PROCRASTINATE

People procrastinate by putting things off rather than working on them. This causes things to build up to the point where they're no longer manageable. As Professor Mason Cooley said, "Procrastination makes easy things hard, hard things harder." Here are 12 reasons why folks procrastinate:

Lack of discipline. "I'll do this some other time."

Fear of failure. "I'm not sure I can do this, so I won't even try."

Wishful thinking. "If I don't think about it, maybe it'll go away."

Unreasonable expectations. "If I can't guarantee success, I won't even attempt it."

Feeling overwhelmed. "This project seems daunting. Let me give it some thought…tomorrow."

Fear of complexity. "I'm not sure where to begin."

Lack of motivation. "I'm not in the mood."

Fear of accountability. "I'm afraid to put my neck on the line."

Feeling bored. "I'd rather be doing something else."

Lack of urgency. "It really doesn't matter if I do it now. It's not due for days."

Fear of making a decision. "I need more information before I can start."

Wait till the last minute. "I love the adrenaline rush that I get when I'm up against a deadline."

Do any of these explanations sound familiar? If so, do something about it — don't procrastinate. Remember, those who begin things, but never complete them, accomplish nothing. :)

I'M NOT SURE
I CAN DO THIS,
SO I WON'T
EVEN TRY.

STOP TRYING TO
CONTROL THE
UNCONTROLLABLE.

42 WAYS TO MAKE YOUR LIFE EASIER

1. Think before you begin.

2. Keep it simple.

3. Let it go. Just let it go.

4. Never be too proud to learn.

5. Be yourself.

6. Value relationships over possessions.

7. Learn to delegate.

8. Leave game playing to fifth graders.

9. Strive for win-win rather than winner takes all.

10. Address small problems before they become big ones.

11. Stop trying to change people who don't want to change.

12. Determine whether it's been done before.

13. Stop overthinking everything.

14. Listen — don't just hear.

15. Choose the right solution rather than the easy one.

16. Tell the truth.

17. Set priorities. Don't treat everything equally.

18. Compete against yourself rather than against others.

19. Don't wait for a fire to locate the exits.

20. Save for a rainy day.

21. Do it right the first time.

22. Shop value rather than price.

23. Never take things for granted.

24. Learn to say "I don't know" and "I was wrong."

25. Focus your efforts instead of trying to be great at everything.

26. Keep your ego in check.

27. Think before you speak.

28. Stop…if your gut says "no."

29. Keep your promises.

30. Keep your problems in perspective.

31. Stop trying to control the uncontrollable.

32. Do preventive maintenance before it becomes an emergency.

33. Know where you're going before trying to get there.

34. Ask for help if you need it.

35. Live within your means.

36. Know your limits.

37. Settle for excellence rather than perfection.

38. Admit mistakes and learn from them.

39. Make a decision and don't look back.

40. Don't say "maybe" when you really want to say "no."

41. Learn the meaning of *enough*.

42. Listen to your conscience. :)

WE CAN'T DO
ANYTHING TO
IMPROVE OUR PAST,
BUT WE CAN LEARN
FROM IT TO IMPROVE
OUR FUTURE.

YOU MAY REGRET
NOT READING THIS

What are your biggest regrets? I asked quite a few folks that question recently. Why? Because we have a choice: We can learn from other people's mistakes or make them ourselves. The answers I received were enlightening.

THE 34 BIGGEST REGRETS IN LIFE
(A NONSCIENTIFIC SURVEY)

1. **Rushing through life.** Some people are always on the run. They're so busy being busy that they fail to make the time to enjoy life.
2. **Moving the finish line.** Some folks place artificial demands on themselves that undermine their happiness. They think greater wealth leads to happiness, so they work harder and harder just to cross a finish line that keeps moving.
3. **Keeping bad company.** Some people let themselves get dragged down by toxic people who lack a moral compass.
4. **Lacking goals.** Some folks take life as it comes, and then seem surprised to see where life has taken them.
5. **Speaking before thinking.** Some people say or text things without thinking and then wish they could take back their words.
6. **Taking things for granted.** Some folks take things for granted and lose them as a result.
7. **Fearing change.** Some people are so afraid of leaving their comfort zone that they let opportunities pass them by.

8. **Failing to say "no."** Some folks want to please others so much that they fail to satisfy their *own* needs.

9. **Failing to see the downside.** Some people rarely consider the downside of an opportunity. They never think the worst will happen — until it does.

10. **Being the life of the party.** Some folks don't realize the damage they can cause themselves by reckless personal behavior.

11. **Covering for the misdeeds of others.** Some people conceal the misdeeds of others and become linked to their wrongdoings.

12. **Following the crowd.** Some folks think others know better...and they follow them right off a cliff.

13. **Worshipping possessions.** Some people view belongings, rather than relationships, as the standard by which success is measured.

14. **Becoming overly dependent.** Some folks become so dependent on others that they lose confidence in themselves and are stripped of their dignity.

15. **Compromising their integrity.** Some people sell their soul to the highest bidder and live with that choice for the rest of their life.

16. **Putting off problems.** Some folks put off problems when they're small, only to see them snowball out of control down the road.

17. **Failing to make hard choices.** Some people treat *everything* as a priority — which means *nothing* is a priority. As a result, important things don't get the attention they deserve.

18. **Letting success go to their head.** Some folks think a comfortable lead can't be lost. So they get sloppy and lose as a result.

19. **Failing to accept personal responsibility.** Some people blame the world for their misfortune and are unwilling to make the effort to achieve success.

20. **Being blinded by jealousy.** Some folks are so obsessed with envy that they let resentment consume them.

21. **Living with fear and anxiety.** Some people spend every waking moment worrying about what might happen. The truth is, it rarely does.

22. **Building walls around themselves.** Some folks are so afraid of getting hurt that they keep relationships at a distance.

23. **Being distrustful.** Some people are so afraid of getting burned that they treat everyone around them as a suspect.

24. **Failing to forgive.** Some folks are so consumed by vengeance that they get swallowed up by their anger and can't let it go.

25. **Talking a good game.** Some people have big dreams, but rarely act on them.

26. **Acting like a control freak.** Some folks try to do *everything* themselves and then wonder why they're always stressed out.

27. **Believing they're Peter Pan.** Some people don't want to grow up, (Then they try to make up for lost time after seeing everyone else in the passing lane.)

28. **Losing the trust of others.** Some folks violate the trust of friends and colleagues and then want things to be the same as they used to be.

29. **Letting themselves down.** Some people have incredible ability but fail to do what it takes to live up to their true potential.

30. **Winning at all costs.** Some folks try to get the upper hand in relationships and seem surprised when that behavior is reciprocated.

31. **Creating self-imposed pressure.** Some people create unrealistic goals and artificial deadlines for themselves, which leads to anxiety and stress.

32. **Choosing the shortcut.** Some folks take the easy route only to learn that it's filled with potholes. The truth is, there are simply no shortcuts in the long term.

33. **Trying to change others.** Some people try to convert others to their way of thinking. The fact is, people change only when change is *their* choice.

34. **Not speaking out against injustice.** Some folks sit silently and wait for others to do the heavy lifting — that is, if anyone does.

Do these regrets sound familiar? What will you start doing differently? As Jackie Joyner-Kersee, the retired American track and field athlete, said, "It's better to look ahead and prepare, than to look back and regret." We can't do anything to improve our past, but we can learn from it to improve our future. :)

IT TAKES MANY
YEARS TO BECOME
AN OVERNIGHT
SUCCESS.

MAKE YOUR DREAMS COME TRUE

Magnificent dreams are within your reach, but it requires more than hope if you want them to come true. The truth is, success won't be served to you on a silver platter or come your way just for the asking. Dreams, unlike eggs, don't hatch from sitting on them.

Here are 14 requirements for turning your dreams into reality:

Take action. Stop procrastinating. Nothing happens until you act.

Prepare to sacrifice. Dreams come with a price tag. Know what you're willing to sacrifice and where you draw the line.

Be passionate. Here's a no-brainer. Follow your heart and don't let your brain talk you out of it.

Stay confident. If you believe you can't, you won't!

Be strong-minded. Once you make a decision, don't look back. Make it work.

Adopt an attitude. Surround yourself with positive people. Their energy is contagious.

Be courageous. Face your challenges head-on rather than surrendering your dreams to fear.

Make good choices. Every choice that you make will steer you either closer to or away from your goals.

Show pride. Do your best. If you're not proud, you're not done.

Build momentum. Set achievable, short-term goals. Small wins will keep you motivated as you pursue your long-term dreams.

Exercise strength. Give it all you've got or don't waste your time.

Be clever. Don't let obstacles get in your way. Turn barriers into hurdles.

Stay the course. It takes many years to become an overnight success.

Be humble. Don't let success go to your head.

Don't wait for the perfect time to pursue your dreams. The truth is, it may never come. As Walt Disney said, "All our dreams can come true — if we have the courage to pursue them." :)

FACE YOUR
CHALLENGES
HEAD-ON
RATHER THAN
SURRENDERING
YOUR DREAMS
TO FEAR.

EVEN THOUGH
IT'S GREAT TO WIN
A GAME, IT'S EVEN
BETTER TO BE A
SUPERSTAR IN LIFE.

WHAT CAN SPORTS TEACH YOUR KIDS ABOUT LIFE?

A re you using every opportunity to prepare your children for the game of life? Take your cue from the great coaches in all sports and at all levels. They use sports to teach their players valuable lessons. Teach your child that success doesn't come easily. Life is a continuing competition in which excellence wins. Therefore, it's better to learn how to compete when the consequences are small. If you aren't using every opportunity to prepare your child for the game of life, your son or daughter is being cheated out of something very special. Even though it's great to win a game, it's even better to be a superstar in life.

25 THINGS THAT SPORTS CAN TEACH YOUR KIDS ABOUT LIFE

1. **Attitude is everything.** Be positive. Set high expectations. Replace negative thinking with a can-do attitude.

2. **Get in the game.** Anyone can watch a game, but winners get off the sidelines and play. Don't let fear of failure stop you from reaching your full potential. Remember, it's better to go down swinging than to be called out on strikes.

3. **Winning is as much mental as physical.** Control your emotions. Stay focused and remain disciplined.

4. **Master the fundamentals.** Practice, practice, practice. When you master the basics, and execute them well, there's no need to worry about the score.

5. **Few things come easy in life.** Success is achieved through hard work and determination. It takes many years to become an overnight success.

6. **Always do your best.** Aim high and never settle for second best. Strive for continuous improvement in everything you do. As Coach Vince Lombardi once said, "Winning is not everything — but making the effort to win is."

7. **Be ready on game day.** Anyone can talk a good game. What matters is what you do when it counts.

8. **Remain flexible and embrace change.** You can't control the uncontrollable. So be prepared to expect the unexpected.

9. **View obstacles as opportunities.** When barriers get in your way, find a way around them and use them to learn and develop. Don't feel sorry for yourself.

10. **Know your strengths and the strengths of others.** Don't try to win games by yourself. Trust and support your teammates and they'll place their faith in you.

11. **Be a team player.** Be prepared to make personal sacrifices for the good of the team.

12. **Keep your perspective.** Competition will test your limits. Be calm, strong, and in control when it matters most.

13. **Be a leader.** Set high standards of excellence for yourself and others. Make people feel special and help bring out the best in everyone.

14. **If you can't play fair, don't play.** Integrity matters. Compete fairly and fully. When you resort to cheating, you've already lost.

15. **Quitting is not an option.** There will be times when things get tough. Always keep hope alive and display confidence in the eye of defeat. As Morgan Freeman said, "The best way to guarantee a loss is to quit."

16. **Accept responsibility for your actions.** You're in the driver's seat. Only you can decide how hard you're willing to work to achieve your goals. If you succeed, the rewards are yours. If you fail, there's always another day.

17. **Learn to forgive.** Forgive the mistakes of others. It may be your error that costs the team tomorrow.

18. **Support others in need.** Real friends are available in good times and bad. So offer your teammates encouragement and support, especially when they have a bad day.

19. **Look to the future rather than the past.** Don't dwell on mistakes or past defeats. Learn from the experience and move on.

20. **Follow directions.** Listen to your coach and respect the call of a referee, even if you disagree.

21. **Compete against yourself.** Competing against others may be destructive if more effort is spent tearing others down than on improving your own game. When you compete against yourself, however, you both win.

22. **Raise your game.** Find a good role model. Don't be shy to ask for help. Be open to feedback and put it to good use.

23. **Say "no" to unhealthy behavior.** Take care of your body. It's the only one you've got.

24. **Know that losing doesn't make you a failure.** Be a good loser. Bounce back after a big loss.

25. **Be a good winner.** Be a winner on and off the field. Be humble and quietly proud but never self-satisfied. And never let success go to your head. :)

PEOPLE NEED ROLE
MODELS. ARE YOU
UP TO THE JOB?

WE'RE ALL TEACHERS

When you're a role model, you are influencing people every day. Be a positive force in their life. Make a difference. Make people feel special; bring out the best in them; help them without expecting something in return; be genuinely happy for their achievements. The more you do for others, the happier you'll be.

Every message you send is critical. Operate with integrity at all times. Do what's right. Period. That way, you'll never have to look over your shoulder to see who's watching. Have high expectations for others AND yourself. Avoid the tendency to adjust the target downward just to accommodate mediocrity. People need role models. Are you up to the job? Here are 40 action items for you to consider:

1. Lead by example.

2. Set the bar high.

3. Live with honor and integrity.

4. Give more than you take.

5. Walk the talk.

6. Pull others up the ladder with you.

7. Surround yourself with top-notch people.

8. Keep your promises to others — and yourself.

9. Be kind and generous.

10. Do your best. Be your best.

11. Earn respect.

12. Listen before you speak.

13. Bring out the best in others.

14. Tell the whole truth.

15. Have faith.

16. Show gratitude.

17. Be open-minded and tolerant.

18. Learn something new.

19. Leave your comfort zone.

20. Be a good friend.

21. Build trust.

22. Show some class.

23. Forgive and forget.

24. Focus on things that matter.

25. Remember your manners.

26. Earn your success.

27. Learn from mistakes and failures.

28. Build good karma.

29. Put family first.

30. Be happy for others' success.

31. Maintain work-life balance.

32. Build win-win relationships.

33. Honor tradition.

34. Remain true to your values.

35. Be humble.

36. Reach for the stars.

37. Remember your roots.

38. Be accountable.

39. Make a difference.

40. Do what's right. Period. :)

KNOWING
WHAT'S RIGHT
ISN'T AS IMPORTANT
AS DOING
WHAT'S RIGHT.

DO YOU CHOOSE CONVENIENCE OVER PRINCIPLES?

We're faced with decisions each day. It's not enough to know the difference between right and wrong. The important thing is to convert those principles into words and actions. Given the option, would you rather choose the *right* path, even though it's difficult, or the *easy* route, knowing that you'll be compromising your standards? The West Point cadet prayer* sums up their position well: "Make us to choose the harder right instead of the easier wrong."

11 WAYS FOLKS CHOOSE CONVENIENCE OVER PRINCIPLES

It may be easier to:

1. Sugarcoat bad news rather than tell it like it is.

2. Sweep a problem under the rug rather than address the issue head-on.

3. Create low expectations rather than set "stretch" goals.

4. Look the other way rather than reprimand a star performer for unethical behavior.

5. Point a finger rather than admit a mistake and learn a valuable lesson.

6. Throw money at a problem rather than make good use of what one has.

7. Follow the crowd rather than remain true to one's beliefs and values.

8. Promote a quick-fix solution rather than address a problem's root cause.

9. Distribute resources equally rather than set priorities and make tough choices.

10. Maintain silence rather than speak up against injustice.

11. Encourage dependency rather than provide people with good opportunities as well as the tools to succeed.

Compromising your principles, even one time, can be a terrible mistake. As the saying goes, "Watch your thoughts, for they become words. Watch your words, for they become actions. Watch your actions, for they become habits. Watch your habits, for they become your character. And watch your character, for it becomes your destiny!" The fact is, knowing what's right isn't as important as doing what's right. **:)**

*https://www.usma.edu/chaplain/sitepages/cadet%20prayer.aspx

COMPROMISING
YOUR PRINCIPLES,
EVEN ONE TIME,
CAN BE A TERRIBLE
MISTAKE.

WHAT CONTRIBUTES
MOST TO YOUR
SUCCESS —
KNOWLEDGE, SKILLS,
EXPERIENCE,
MINDSET, OR
CHARACTER?

50 QUESTIONS TO UNLOCK YOUR POTENTIAL

1. Do you define *success* differently than *happiness?*

2. Do you follow your own advice?

3. Are you excited to get up in the morning?

4. Do you listen to your conscience?

5. Do you make — or *let* — things happen?

6. How high do you set the bar for yourself?

7. Do you make yourself proud?

8. Do you think "everybody does it" is a valid excuse for poor behavior?

9. What percentage of your worries actually comes to pass?

10. What areas of your life are out of balance?

11. Do you bring out the best in people?

12. Do you value possessions more than relationships?

13. Would you be happy if your kids mimicked your behavior?

14. Do you accept responsibility or make excuses?

15. Do you deserve other people's respect?

16. Would *you* be friends with *you*?

17. Are you better at giving advice or taking it?

18. Do you keep promises that you make to others — and to yourself?

19. What contributes most to your success — knowledge, skills experience, mindset, or character?

20. Do you ask more of others than you're willing to do yourself?

21. Do you invest your time or spend it?

22. Are you a fair-weather friend?

23. What's holding you back?

24. How much time do you spend thinking versus doing?

25. Do you compete more with yourself or with others?

26. How much would you forgo to ensure a better future for your kids?

27. Do you spend more time looking forward or backward?

28. Do you value other people's opinions more than your own?

29. Do you spend more time talking or listening?

30. Is the grass greener on *your* side of the fence?

31. Is learning a priority for you?

32. Do you surround yourself with toxic or honorable people?

33. Do you spend more time living in the present or reliving the past?

34. How much time do you spend doing what you *have to* versus what you *want to?*

35. Do you do your best *some* or *most* of the time?

36. Is your ego bigger than your accomplishments?

37. Do you take things for granted?

38. Do you rely more on others or on yourself?

39. What would you have done differently now that you know?

40. Do you put other people's interests ahead of your own?

41. Do you accept responsibility for the choices that you make?

42. What would it take for you to compromise your integrity?

43. Are you more talk or more action?

44. Do you enjoy your own company?

45. Do you collect things or moments?

46. Do you actively try to better yourself?

47. Do you learn from your mistakes?

48. Do you give more than you take?

49. Are you a good role model?

50. Would you rather be remembered for what you have or who you are? :)

OWN YOUR LIFE!

EVERYONE IS BORN WITH THE
POTENTIAL FOR GREATNESS.
WHAT HAPPENS NEXT IS UP TO YOU.
YOU GET TO CHOOSE WHICH PATH YOU
TAKE, HOW HIGH TO SET THE BAR FOR
YOURSELF, AND HOW HARD YOU'RE
WILLING TO WORK TO CLEAR IT.
YOU GET TO DECIDE HOW TO SPEND
YOUR TIME, WHO TO SPEND IT WITH,
AND WHAT YOU'RE WILLING TO FORGO
WHEN TIME RUNS SHORT.
EVERY CHOICE THAT YOU MAKE
AND EVERY ACTION THAT YOU TAKE
HAS CONSEQUENCES, BUT WHO
BETTER TO DECIDE WHAT'S BEST
FOR YOU — THAN YOU?
IT'S YOUR LIFE TO LIVE. OWN IT!

— FRANK SONNENBERG

ABOUT THE AUTHOR

Frank Sonnenberg is an award-winning author. He has written seven books and over 300 articles. Frank was recently named one of "America's Top 100 Thought Leaders" and one of "America's Most Influential Small Business Experts." Frank has served on several boards and has consulted to some of the largest and most respected companies in the world.

Additionally, *FrankSonnenbergOnline* was named among the "Best 21st Century Leadership Blogs"; among the "Top 100 Socially-Shared Leadership Blogs"; and one of the "Best Inspirational Blogs On the Planet."

OTHER TITLES FROM FRANK SONNENBERG

BOOKSMART
Hundreds of Real-World Lessons for Success and Happiness

Follow Your Conscience
Make a Difference in Your Life & in the Lives of Others

Managing with a Conscience (Second Edition)
How to Improve Performance Through Integrity,
Trust, and Commitment

It's the Thought That Counts
Over 100 Thought-Provoking Lessons to Inspire a Richer Life

Marketing to Win
Strategies for Building Competitive Advantage in Service Industries

Made in the USA
Middletown, DE
19 December 2018